# Step-by-Step Pyrography Projects

*for the Solid Point Machine*

# Step-by-Step Pyrography Projects

## *for the Solid Point Machine*

Norma Gregory

Guild of Master Craftsman Publications

First published 2000 by
Guild of Master Craftsman Publications Ltd,
166 High Street, Lewes,
East Sussex BN7 1XU

ISBN 0 186108 183 9

Editor: Nicola Wright
Copy editor: Philip De Ste Croix
Photographer: Anthony Bailey
Designed by Fineline Studios
Cover designer: Richard Peters
Typeface: Minion
Colour separation: Viscan Graphics Pte Ltd (Singapore)
Printed by Sun Fung Offset Binding Co. Ltd, China

10 9 8 7 6 5 4 3 2 1

*To my husband, Dennis, with love*

# Acknowledgements

Nearly 20 years ago I was given a pyrograph machine by my husband, Dennis, who thought I might like to give it a try. I did, learning from my mistakes, as there was little instructional information available then. To him goes a big thank you for all his encouragement and support over the years. Thanks are also due to Longridge Library (Lancashire) who gave me my first exhibition of pokerwork and who were so helpful. Thank you to Adrian Adamson and the Craft and Design Technology Workshop inmates of HMP Littlehey, Cambridgeshire, who made most of the wooden items that I have pyrographed for this book, and who were such excellent students of pyrography. Finally, thank you to all those at home and abroad who have purchased my work and entrusted me with their special commissions.

# CONTENTS

# INTRODUCTION

Pyrography, the art of 'drawing with fire', is a very ancient craft that is practised worldwide. Mainly used to burn decorative marks onto wooden items, the technique has also been applied to leather, cork, velvet and other suitable materials. Pyrographed artefacts embodying traditional and religious designs are still an integral part of many folk cultures. During the Victorian period, the craft really captured the popular imagination. Initially the work was rather crude, relying as it did simply on using the poker from the fire. The term 'pokerwork' became synonymous with work of inferior quality.

Not satisfied with such poor results, Victorian practitioners developed a series of fine steel rods, rather like steel knitting needles. These were heated in a fire or over a spirit lamp. These finer 'pokers' enabled the pyrographer to work more skillfully and to produce a far superior product. The instruments still had one major drawback, however; they did not retain their heat for long. Work was seriously disrupted because the rods had to be constantly reheated. By the turn of the century, a continuously heated machine had appeared on the market – 'The Vulcan'(see below). At the same time a wide range of wooden items were being manufactured specifically for the pyrographer.

For the first time, a machine was available which supplied a constant heat and provided a variety of interchangeable nibs/points. These advances improved techniques and the quality of the finished work. Let us look at the Vulcan in a little more detail. This 'Burntwood' etching machine made by Messrs Abbott Brothers of Southall was supplied in a neat wooden box and contained all that the pyrographer required for a price ranging from eight shillings and sixpence to sixteen shillings (the equivalent of 42½ pence up to 80 pence in the UK today, not allowing for inflation!). The box contained two glass bottles – a little like scent bottles – the point(s) (made of platinum), the point holder, a rubber ball and rubber tubing, junctions, fittings and benzoline – a highly inflammable liquid.

The bottle was stopped with a rubber-collared metal stopper. From this stopper ran two rubber tubes. One went to the hollow, cork-padded holder which had a screw-in platinum point, the other to the rubber ball which acted as a bellows. When the ball was squeezed, air was pushed through the liquid benzoline, mixing with the gas being given off, and forcing this gas down the hollow tube through the inside of the holder to the platinum point. The point was pre-heated in a flame. When the gas reached the point, it

*The Vulcan*

*What remains of a Vulcan machine owned by the author, the rubber tubes and ball having perished*

ignited so heating the point. Keeping the point supplied with gas ensured that it was continuously heated. I have in my possession a glass bottle, stopper and point holder from one of these machines. Sadly, the rubber tubes and ball have long since perished.

After the Vulcan, the development of the poker progressed through the soldering-iron type to the electric machines we know today. It is interesting that the present holders are very similar in size and shape to the venerable Vulcan, even down to screw-in interchangeable points.

This book deals entirely with the Janik G4 solid-point machine, and the Universal 21 point, which I prefer to the wire-point machine. Many of my students, having tried both, also prefer the solid point because of the delicacy of line it is capable of producing. As you work through the projects in this book, you will gradually build up a repertoire of techniques which you can use to interpret any subject, from border designs to wildlife, from lettering to floral designs, or any other motif that is of interest to you.

I hope that, as you work your way through the book, you acquire some useful hints and tips and catch a glimpse of my love and enthusiasm for pyrography. Over the last 20 years or so, I have enjoyed it so much! Sharing my knowledge and skills with others has been a large part of that enjoyment, and I am still actively involved in teaching these skills to others, many of whom have never done anything artistic in their lives. It never ceases to amaze me how skilful the vast majority of these students become. Even more surprising and satisfying are the different styles of pyrography produced by them. The machine used, the design being worked and the techniques used may be the same, but the end results are so very different from student to student.

I hope this book will encourage you to carry on and develop your skills still further. Your use of the pyrograph, the techniques you use and the style you develop will be yours and yours alone. If, at the same time, it contributes to the development of the craft and its recognition as an art in its own right, then my efforts will not have been wasted.

There are no set rules – it is up to you to push the frontiers of the craft as far as your own skills and imaginations will allow. Enjoy it!

# PYROGRAPHY EQUIPMENT

There are various kinds of pyrography machines available to suit most budgets. I shall describe the most important variants in some detail.

## The soldering iron type

This looks like a soldering iron but is designed for multicraft use. However, I do know of people who have used these for pokerwork. They tend to have larger points and consequently produce a cruder line. This type of 'poker' does not reach the necessary level of heat required to produce a good burned line. There are, however, similar-looking poker pens which are made specifically for pokerwork. These plug directly into the electrical mains and consist of a length of flex and a holder, which has a small screw near the point end. This can be loosened to enable the point to be removed and exchanged for another. The screw is then tightened again to hold the point secure. The main disadvantage is that you cannot regulate the heat, and the points tend to be rather thick. The poker pen is also longer and heavier than the holders provided by the manufacturers of specialist machines.

**Janik Pyro 140** This is a new addition to the range of pyrographs. It looks like a soldering iron, but has been designed specifically by Janik for pyrography. It is provided with its own stand and two double-ended points.

*Holder for the Janik G4 solid point machine fitted with a Universal 21 point*

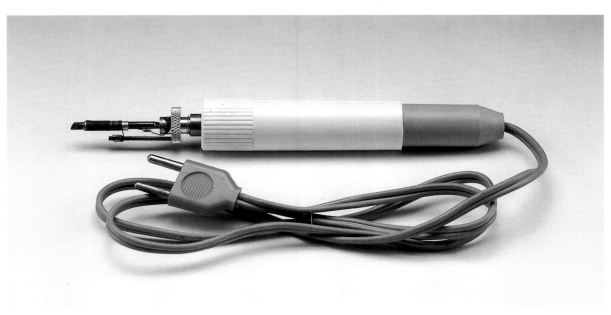

# Hot-wire type

As the name implies, the point is made of a loop of nickel chromium wire, similar to fuse wire. A small length is cut off the reel and bent into a 'wishbone' shape, the stalk being the part that is directly in contact with the surface of the wood. The open branches of the 'wishbone' are held between two screw terminals in the holder. The main advantage of this type of poker is the cheapness of the points. With the help of a pair of fine-nose pliers, you can easily form the wire into any shape you want. This is a good machine, but personally I prefer the solid point, as I can achieve a finer quality of line. Stephen Poole's book *The Complete Pyrography* comprehensively covers the use of the hot-wire machine.

# Solid point type

All the work and the instructions given in this book are for the solid point poker. My preferred choice is the Janik G4. The solid point poker has a solid metal point with its own heating element located close to the tip. The points are screwed into the top of the special plastic holder. This is then connected by a flex and a plug to a transformer, which plugs into the mains. There is a wide variety of points available from suppliers including a complete set of alphabet brands. I have tried some of these specialist points, for example the shading one, but I prefer to use the Universal 21 point for all my work.

# Basic equipment

**Pencils** Use HB for general drawing and design work, particularly when drawing directly onto the surface of the wood. A harder pencil, H or 2H, is better for tracing the design onto the wood as it has a much harder lead.

**Eraser** Use a soft eraser to remove pencil lines, rather than a hard plastic one.

*Basic pyrography equipment*

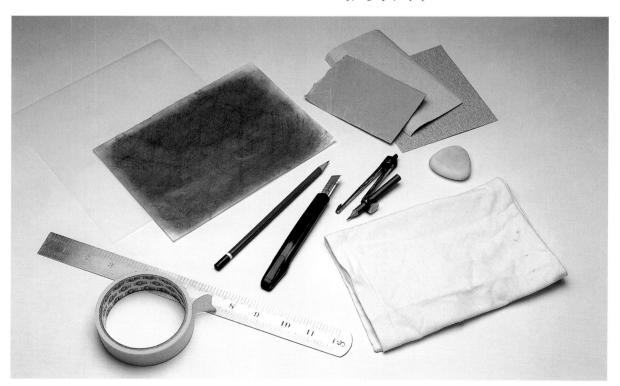

**Steel ruler** Not wooden! You may wish to use it to run the nib of the hot poker along its length to make a straight line.

**Compass**

**Masking tape** Low tack to fix your tracings securely onto the wood surface.

**Pencil sharpener or a sharp pointed knife** You need to keep a very good point on your pencils when drawing or tracing your design. A sharp pointed knife is also very useful for removing mistakes, by carefully scraping away the burned area.

**Tracing paper** Buy a good quality one which will let you see a clear, sharp outline when it is placed over your chosen design.

**Carbon paper or home-made graphite paper** This is used under your traced design to transfer it onto the wood. Graphite paper, which is made from rubbed-on pencil lead, produces marks which are much easier to remove than those made by carbon paper (see page 61 which explains how to make your own).

**Medium and fine sandpaper** Used to prepare the wood prior to transferring your design onto it.

**Varnish** Either gloss or satin, according to how you like the finish on your work.

**Table lamp** Preferably with an adjustable head to illuminate your work clearly.

**Cotton cloth** For applying the varnish. The cloth must be lint-free. You can, of course, use a brush, but I prefer to use a cloth rag so that no loose hairs are left in the varnish.

# Working safely

Before you begin, it is important to make sure that you take reasonable precautions so that you will work safely. Used responsibly, modern machines are usually quite safe. However, it is essential to follow simple safety guidelines.

- Do not touch the point while the machine is plugged in and hot.
- Do not interfere with the transformer unit, nor try to poke anything into it.
- Always unplug the machine and allow the point to cool before changing it.
- Avoid getting the flex twisted or using it where it constantly rubs against another surface. Both of

these eventualities could expose the wires in the flex.
- Do not store the machine with the flex wrapped around anything.
- Some woods, cork and leather may give off nasty fumes and smells when heat is applied to them. Always work in a well-ventilated room.
- Do not work with the unit where it might be exposed to damp, rain or water of any kind.
- Treat anything electrical with the greatest respect and use your common sense.
- Wear a mask when sanding MDF and hardwoods, as the dust from these can be harmful.

# Woods

A wide selection of suitable woods is available from specialist pyrography blank suppliers. The blanks come in all sorts of shapes, sizes and prices. However, these are very expensive to practise on! While you are getting to know your poker, you may find it cheaper to practise on plywood offcuts, which you can obtain from your local joiner or DIY store. Look for plywood which is very light in colour and as smooth-grained as possible. Birch ply is best – but this is more expensive than ordinary plywood. Always sand any wood with fine sandpaper before you begin. Follow the direction of the grain as you sand and always clean off the dust after you have sanded it. Once you have mastered the basic pyrography techniques, you will need a good wood to show off your work to its best advantage. You will find the English hardwoods lovely to work on and easy to find.

Sycamore, beech and birch are English hardwoods that are very dense, fine-grained and light in colour. This pale background shows off the burned lines extremely well. Most firms supplying blanks use these woods. Other suitable varieties are lime, hornbeam and holly. Woods such as teak, oak, and mahogany can be used but they are darker in colour and have a more pronounced grain. The smoother the grain, the finer and more delicate your work will be. Pine, while easily available, is a very soft wood and the burns produced tend to be dark with thick lines, which have a crusty deposit around them.

From time to time you may need a much larger piece of wood than you can obtain in blanks. Birch

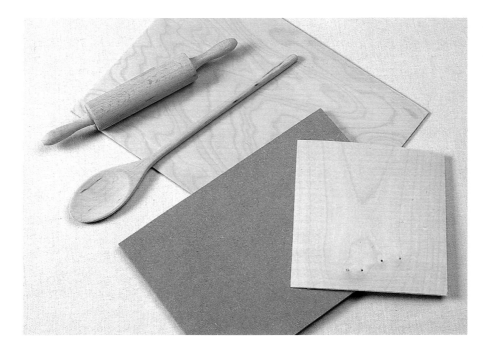

*Light-coloured wood or veneer is best for pyrography. For example, beech, birch, hornbeam and sycamore*

ply is ideal for this, as it has a lovely finish and is light in colour, rather like sycamore. You may need to visit a specialist wood yard to find this.

# Veneers

Solid boxes made of sycamore, beech or similar woods are expensive. It is cheaper to make boxes and other items as blanks in MDF (medium-density fibreboard) and then cover them with a veneer of sycamore, holly or lime. Veneer is easy to work but you must remember that it is only a very thin sheet of wood applied to a base – so don't burn too deeply!

Most woods, including veneers, have lovely grain patterns. Look closely at these before you decide on your design – the grain itself may suggest water, cloud, or hill effects. You can use these to enhance your work.

# BASIC TECHNIQUES

T he most important thing to remember when you begin is that 'practice makes perfect' and 'patience is a virtue'! You will need plenty of both if you want to be pleased with your results. It is worth the time and the effort at this stage to practise as much as you can on plywood offcuts. The exercises should be done using the solid point Janik G4 with the Universal 21 point. Ready?

## Exercise 1

Plug the machine into the mains and set the heat control to 12 o'clock. Wait a short while until the point warms up. Think of your poker as a 'hot' pencil producing brown lines instead of grey ones. There is no right or wrong way to hold it, but you must feel comfortable while using it.

First, practise drawing a few lines of varying lengths by placing the point with its fine thin edge onto the surface of the wood. Do not press on, but smoothly pull the point over the surface towards you. Aim to keep the movement of the point continuous from the beginning to the end of the line.

No hesitations now! If you do pause, you will see a darker patch on the line where you hesitated. This is not necessarily a problem, but there will be times when you want to produce a continuous line with a uniform colour from start to finish. As you will use line quite a lot for outlining your designs, it is important that you can produce a line with a nice, even tone. Go on, have another try – it's worth it!

## Exercise 2

Now that you have mastered the first exercise, try to angle the point slightly over to the right as you draw the lines again. By leaning the point, more of its surface area comes into contact with the wood. This produces a broader line. With practice, you will soon learn how far to angle the point to the right to produce the width of line you want. It is very useful to be able to vary the width of the line as you make it. Practise drawing a line beginning with the fine edge on the wood. As you draw it over the surface, lean the point over to the right. Do not hesitate as you change the angle of the point. Now that you can draw lines of reasonable lengths really well and with control, let us look at using line for shading.

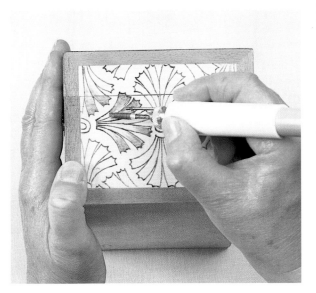

*Left: Outlining and shading an overall pattern*

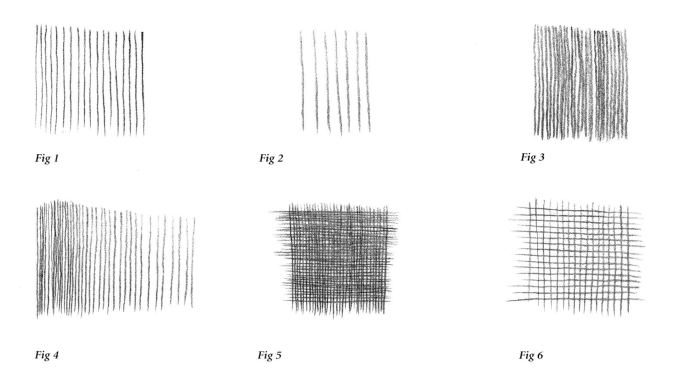

Fig 1

Fig 2

Fig 3

Fig 4

Fig 5

Fig 6

## Exercise 3 – types of shading

**Hatching** As with a pencil, you use a series of lines set closely together to form areas of shade (Fig 1). In Fig 2 the lines are spaced further apart and produce an area of lighter-looking tone. Fig 3 looks darker because the lines are drawn closer together; in Fig 4 the lines start close together, and then move further apart giving an area of graded tone. It is this skilful use of dark, medium and light areas that will enable you to enhance your work and give emphasis to the most important parts of your design.

**Cross-hatching** Another common pencil and engraving technique, this involves drawing one set of lines at an angle across another set of lines. In Fig 5

the cross-hatching is set close together giving an area of dark tone while in Fig 6 the lines are more widely spaced, giving a lighter tone. Now practise these techniques on your piece of plywood.

## Exercise 4 – stippling with dots

As with hatching (lines), the dot can also be used very effectively. It takes a little longer as the dots need to be carefully placed for a satisfactory result. Use the very tip of your point, and carefully place the dots as closely together as you can. This will give you a dark area (Fig 7). Space them further apart and this will give you a lighter area (Fig 8). In Fig 9 the dots are placed close together at the top and then are

Fig 7

Fig 8

Fig 9

*Right: Sampler showing a range of basic pyrography techniques – see key below*

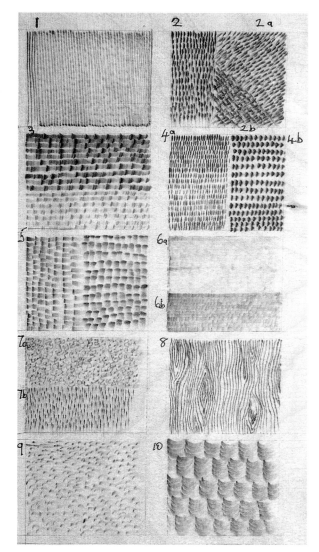

gradually spaced out to give a lighter area towards the bottom. This graded tone is a useful technique to master. Look at the samples you did in Exercise 2. You may find these useful for shading too.

# Exercise 5 – speed

This may seem an unusual 'technique' but control over your speed is a most useful additional skill to have. The slower you pull your point over the surface of the wood, the longer it stays in one place. This produces a darker burn. The faster you pull it over the surface, the less contact it has with the wood, giving a lighter burn mark. So by varying the speed you increase the number of shades of brown you can create. You can add to these by adjusting the heat setting on the machine. Try all the exercises at a low heat, with the control set to, say, 11 o'clock, and then try them again at 1 o'clock. Compare the results with those you achieved when the machine was set at 12 o'clock.

Now that you can use lines, let your imagination run away with you and see how many different kinds of burn marks you can create with the point. Some may look like the examples in the photograph here. Now – have you practised enough? Are you ready for your first piece of work?

## Sampler key using 21 point only

*1  Straight lines using point leaning over slightly to the right.*

*2  Flick down by placing point on surface, hold for a second then flick and lift in a downwards movement.*

*2a Flicks placed diagonally.*

*2b Flicks crossing each other.*

*3  Wash stroke starting with the heat high. Place point on surface, lean over to right, pause then pull smoothly, pause again. Repeat as you go across the line. If you then lower the heat, the effect is paler.*

*4a Using point held vertically with the fine edge on the surface, press in slightly. Repeat side by side.*

*4b Using point lean it over to the right and press into the surface.*

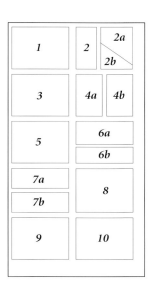

*5  Place point on surface, lean over to the right. Hold then short drag stroke. Repeat.*

*6a Wash, place point on surface and lean over to right. Pull smoothly and quickly over the surface. Repeat in bands.*

*6b Same technique but done slowly.*

*7a Do wash first, place point on surface and take it for a walk all over the wash. Use curling lines.*

*7b Wash first then short flick strokes over it.*

*8  Lines of varying shapes arranged together to simulate wood grain.*

*9  Curling flick strokes at angles to each other.*

*10 Curving wash stroke. Place point on surface, lean to right and pull, using a curving stroke. Start each stroke slowly, the quickly lift off.*

# PROJECT 1
# COMMEMORATIVE SPOONS

M ost commemorative spoons celebrate special occasions in one's life, such as a wedding, anniversary, christening, birthday or exam success. I am sure you will be able to think of many more special events when a personalized spoon would make a welcome gift.

Here are some more ideas:

- Specific fund-raising events
- Charity spoons
- Souvenir spoons featuring places or buildings of note

Ordinary wooden baking spoons are ideal for pyrographing and can be found in most hardware and kitchen shops. You can also purchase them from suppliers of pyrography blanks. Most of them are made from hornbeam, a very light-coloured wood. The spoons can vary in bowl size and handle length. Choose carefully, looking for a good bowl shape and a handle about 300mm (12in) long.

# Wedding spoon

## Tools and materials

Pyrograph with Universal 21 point
Wooden spoon
H or HB pencil
Black carbon or graphite paper
Fine sandpaper
Design (either from the design section of this book or from other sources, such as greetings cards, wrapping paper, or see my first book, *Pyrography Designs*)
Varnish (satin or gloss, depending on your personal taste)

## Method

**1**

Sand the handle and the bowl with fine sandpaper, rubbing with the grain. Draw your design directly into the bowl if you can. If you cannot, there are other ways of transferring your design to the bowl of the spoon. If the design lends itself, cut it out, place it in the bowl and draw round it. Alternatively, place a small bowl-size piece of carbon/graphite paper (shiny side down) in the bowl. Position your design on top of it, and draw over the outlines with a hard pencil. Remove the carbon paper and the design. Another method is to trace a design from the design section. Place a piece of tracing paper over the selected design and draw over the lines carefully. When all the lines are drawn, remove the tracing paper (check that you have traced everything you need to before doing this). Place the tracing over the

carbon paper in the bowl of the spoon and draw over the outlines as described earlier.

**2**

Plug in the pyrograph and let it heat up. Burn over the pencil lines of your design. Remember to use a continuous line, keeping it as fine as you can. You may want to add shading. Look at your original design as this may give you an idea where to place it most effectively. You can use cross-hatching, hatching, stippling or all of these techniques.

**3**

Round the bottom rim of the spoon bowl you can add the date of the wedding and inscribe the name of the church around the top edge (Fig 1). Further personal touches, such as the couple's initials can be placed on the bells or elsewhere, if the design allows. They can also be situated at the bottom of the handle where it opens out into the bowl (Fig 2). Other individual touches could reflect their hobbies or interests. Any extra additions need to look an integral part of the design, so do take care when you add them. They should improve the look of the spoon.

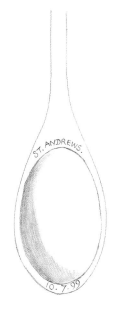

*Fig 1*

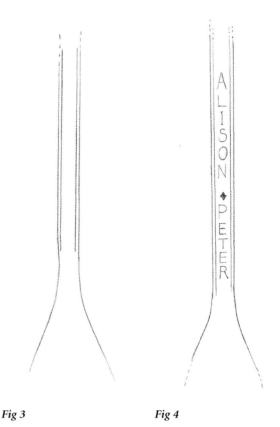

*Fig 2*                                    *Fig 3*                    *Fig 4*

# Lettering the spoon handle

Poor lettering can spoil a good piece of pokerwork. A simple rule is to make all the letters you use uniform – either all capitals or all lowercase letters. If you are good at calligraphy, then you can design your own style. Lettering down the handle of a spoon is made a little more difficult because of its curve. You must hold the spoon steady and flat on your work surface with the bowl facing you.

## Method

**1**

Using your pencil and a ruler, lightly draw two parallel lines down the edges of the centre front panel of the handle (Fig 3). Keep them as wide apart as you can, to allow you plenty of room in which to shape your letters.

**2**

Leaving at least 38mm (1½in) from the top of the handle, write the names in pencil between the lines. Make sure you leave a uniform space between each letter and that the letters are all the same size.

**3**

Leave a larger space after you have completed the first name. Now inscribe the second. I find it useful to put some kind of 'stop' between the two words to distinguish them from one another (Fig 4).

**4**

You may find it a good idea to practise your lettering on some plywood scraps before you start to letter the spoon. Once you have drawn the letters, go over the pencil lines with your point.

*Fig 5*

*Fig 6*

## Useful points to remember

- Keep all the horizontal lines on letters such as E and F the same length (Fig 5).
- Do not put a dot over a capital I.
- The letter S looks better if you make its head smaller than its lower half (Fig 6).
- If you do any lettering on plates or pictures, rule guidelines in pencil for the top and bottom of your letters before you begin.

Once you have finished the lettering and pyrographed it, you can varnish the handle and bowl to protect your work and keep it clean. I apply varnish with a small pad of lint-free cotton cloth (see 'Finishing off the work' on page 63). Your spoon should be looking good now, and only in need of a little appropriate decoration to make it extra special.

# To trim a wedding spoon

## Tools and materials

Pyrographed spoon
1m (3ft) of 13mm (½in) ribbon (white or any other suitable colour)
Assorted small silk or dried flowers and leaves to match (try to vary the size of flower heads for interest)
Household glue
Scissors
Florist's wire

*Tools and materials required for trimming a wedding spoon*

*Fig 7*

*Fig 8*

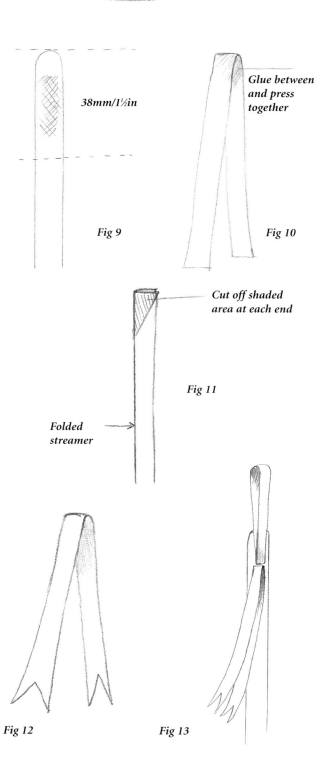

## Method

**1**

Cut two pieces of ribbon off your length, one 152mm (6in) and one 400mm (16in) long. Put the remaining piece to one side to use later.

**2**

Take the 400mm (16in) length, and fold it in half (Fig 7). Slightly overlap and glue the cut ends together to form a loop using a small amount of glue (Fig 8). Be careful with the glue! Leave to dry.

**3**

Smear a small amount of glue onto the back of the handle, spreading the glue along the top 25 to 38mm (1–1½in) of the handle (Fig 9). Press the glued section of your ribbon loop onto this, making sure the loop extends above the top of the spoon. Leave to dry.

**4**

Take the piece of ribbon you previously set aside. Fold it in half and put a small dab of glue between the two halves where you have folded them over (Fig 10). Press together and leave to dry. When dry, fold longitudinally and trim the ends (Fig 11) to form an inverted 'V' shape (Fig 12).

**5**

Dab a small amount of glue onto the back of this ribbon, just below the fold. Press this ribbon streamer onto the back of the spoon, slightly below where you attached the ribbon loop (Fig 13). Allow to dry.

*Fig 14*

*Fig 15*

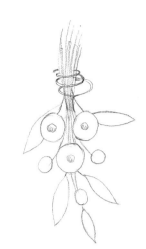

**6**

Take your silk or dried flowers and choose three large ones, two small ones and three or four leaves. Arrange them into a group, as if you were making a spray to pin on your lapel (Fig 14). Take one of the flower stems and wind this tightly around the others to hold them together. If you are using plastic-stemmed silk flowers, then bind all the stems together with a florist's wire (Fig 15).

**7**

Trim the wire stems level with each other, making sure you leave plenty of spare wire above the arrangement. You will need this to fasten the spray to the handle.

**8**

Keeping the back of the spoon flat on your work surface, place the spray along the left side of the handle with the wire stems lying along the top 25 to 38mm (1–1½in) of it. Take the 152mm (6in) piece of ribbon and sparingly smear it with glue all the way along its back. While it is still tacky, hold the wire stems of the spray against the top section of the handle. The bowl should be facing you. Wind your length of glued ribbon tightly round the stems and the handle, rather like a bandage (Fig 16). Make sure it covers the ends of your loop and the 'streamer' joins – these should not be visible (Fig 17). Leave to dry.

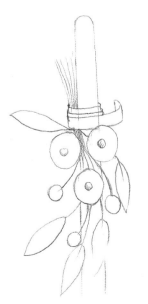

*Fig 16*

*Fig 17*

9

When the ribbon is dry, look at the spoon and, if necessary, shape the flowers by bending the stems gently, so that they drape nicely down the side of the handle. Your spoon is now finished, making a personal memento to celebrate someone's very special occasion.

I have sent personalized spoons all over this country and abroad. If you can make them well and have a good range of designs at your fingertips, then you may wish to consider setting up a postal personalized spoon service. When you decide on a price for them, do not forget to add the post, packing and advertising costs and your profit margin on to your fixed costs. The basic techniques you have used while creating your spoon will certainly encourage you to try other things.

# Design sources

Keep your designs as simple as possible, and concentrate on producing quality linework and good shading. The more complicated they are, and the longer they take to do, the more you will have to charge to cover your costs and allow you a profit margin. This is very important when running a mail-order service. It has to be viable. You should also begin to assemble a reference library of designs. You can find ideas for designs from all kinds of sources: greetings cards, books on wood carving and engraving, wrapping paper, wildlife magazines, country living and home periodicals, gardening magazines, art books, calligraphy books and such like. You can also take your own photographs of buildings, gardens and animals.

The choice is virtually endless. If you can draw, you can sketch on visits to wildlife parks, pretty villages, etc. File your source material away so that you can find it easily. You may need to alter the size of your design – this is easily done on a photocopying machine at a small cost. Keep the copies! There are also books of designs available, specifically for pokerwork (see Bibliography). In fact you can find inspiration for your work in the most unexpected places! Remember to check the copyright on them before you use them, however, as it is illegal to use copyright material without permission.

*You can find ideas for designs from nature and pictures*

# PROJECT 2
# COMMEMORATIVE PLATES

A s with spoons, plates and platters can be pyrographed to commemorate special events, in this case a birth. Because events such as these are so special, they should have designs specific to them. The church where a wedding or christening was held makes a good starting point for such a design. Remember to include important names, dates and place.

## Tools and materials

Pyrograph with Universal 21 point
Design (from design section)
Beech or sycamore platter or rim plate
   (approximately 250mm/10in in diameter)
HB pencil
Carbon or graphite paper
Tracing paper
Masking tape (low tack)
Varnish
Lint-free cloth

If you are using a plate without a rim, you will need to establish a margin all the way round it. This allows you to write in any names and dates you would like to record. Getting the border the same width all the way round can be difficult. Unless you know exactly where the centre of the plate was when it was being turned, you cannot find this point again easily once it is removed from the machine and finished.

## Method

**1**

Lightly sand the surface using the fine sandpaper. Sand with the grain and remove the dust.

**2**

Cut a narrow strip of card (postcard), just under 13mm (½in) wide and about 50mm (2in) long. Mark a line across the strip about 25mm (1in) down from the narrow top edge (Fig 1).

**3**

Place the narrow edge of the card against the outer edge of the plate. Make sure the edge of the card is level with the edge of the plate with the marked line marking the width of the margin 25mm (1in), lying on the plate. Using a pencil, make a mark on the plate in line with the mark on the card. Move the strip of card, in small steps, around the plate keeping the top edge level with the outside rim of the plate. Mark the plate each time you move the card (Fig 2).

**4**

Continue like this until you have worked all round the plate. You should now have a ring of small pencil marks. Join them up to make a continuous circular line.

I find that this method enables me to be quite accurate and it copes with the variations in a plate caused by turning a wooden blank on a lathe. For a plate with a rim, you need only take heed of step 1.

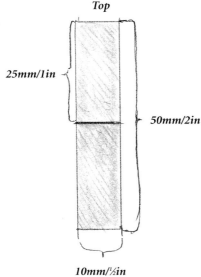

*Top*

*25mm/1in*

*50mm/2in*

*10mm/½in*

**Fig 1**

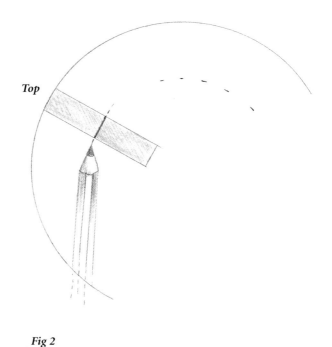

*Top*

**Fig 2**

# Method for completing both plates

Instructions in this section are general hints only on how to prepare a typical design for a birth or christening plate. The church depicted here will, of course, be different from the one that will feature on your plate; however, it was created using only the techniques outlined on pages 7–9.

**1**

Trace off your design. If you can draw it directly onto the plate, then do so. If you want to feature a church and find them difficult to draw, take a photograph, then photocopy it. Enlarge this if necessary to fit the plate and then trace from it.

**2**

Transfer the design to the plate by placing a piece of graphite paper on the plate where the design is to go. Position the traced design over this in the place it is to occupy and attach both pieces of paper to the plate with small pieces of masking tape.

**3**

Inscribe any names or dates in the margin area. You may wish to plan this step first in rough form on a piece of paper the same size as your plate and with the same width of margin indicated on it.

**4**

Using a sharp pencil, draw carefully over your design – do not press too hard, just sufficiently for a faint line to be seen. Check that you have traced down all the details you need before removing the carbon and tracing paper.

**5**

Warm up the pyrograph with its 21 point. Set the heat control at 12 o'clock if your machine has a temperature regulator. Keeping the point in as vertical a position as possible to ensure a fine line, carefully draw over the outlines. To do this accurately, you may find that you will have to move the plate around so that it is easier to work in its well.

**6**

Burn over the names and the dates in the rim or margin of the plate. Try to keep a steady hand and an even burn.

On the plate illustrated on page 17, the shadows on the tower were made using cross-hatching. The shadows under the edges of the rooflines were created by leaning the point over to the right, which gives a broader line. Brick- and stonework is suggested by lines drawn in the shape of bricks (Fig 4) or random stone (Fig 3). You do not need to repeat this all over the building, unless it is a close-up view. Drawing in every brick can look too fussy and overwhelm the design.

*Fig 3*                    *Fig 4*

*Fig 5*                                                                    *Fig 6*

Trees and shrubs on the plate were drawn using stipple dots of varying shades of brown. Where there are shadows, the stipples are set very close together and sometimes overlapping each other. If you leave the point on a little longer than usual, you will get a very dark burn. For the yew trees, I used short lines, again laid over one another (Fig 6). The open-looking tree on the left of the tower was made with stipples of varying sizes (Fig 5). Note that parts of the plate are left unworked here to make the foliage of the trees look more open.

The outline of the clouds was created with stipple and short lines. In the traditional way of engraving, the sky around the clouds was drawn in using broken lines of varying lengths. When the design is completed to your satisfaction, you can apply the finish of your choice.

All commemorative and special occasion plates should have designs appropriate to that event. The church illustrated on this plate was the one at which a baby called Alastair was christened. As you master other techniques, you can of course use these to help interpret your designs.

# MORE USEFUL TECHNIQUES

In this section, I will describe other ways of using your poker to achieve different surface marks, so extending your range of skills. You may have found while using your point that it is not giving you a good line. This can be due to a sooty ash deposit that builds up on the tip of the point as the wood is being burned. To keep your point working well, you must keep cleaning this off. Use a small piece of very fine sandpaper, fold it to make a small pad and very gently stroke this over the deposit to remove it. Always stroke in just one direction. Do not do this when the machine is switched on or still hot.

## Shading – using a wash technique

Shading evenly over a large area is one of the most difficult skills to master, as the finished result needs to look uniform. This requires a good working knowledge of your point and plenty of practice. Don't be put off if the result looks uneven – have another go. It took me quite a lot of attempts to be able to do exactly what I wanted to with this technique. You can use a special shading point, but I prefer to use the Universal 21.

Using a piece of scrap plywood, set your heat regulator to 12 o'clock and allow the point to warm up. Place the sharp edge of the point (where the two sloping sides meet) onto the surface of the wood,

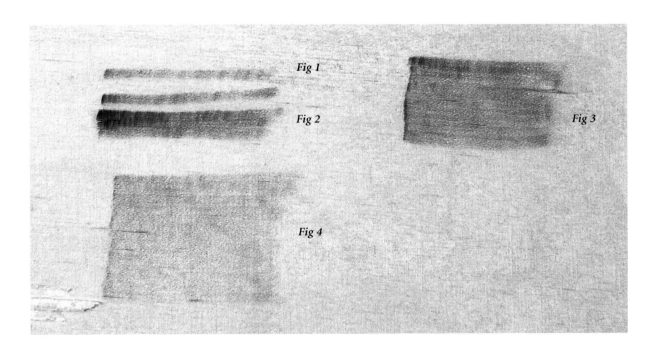

Fig 1

Fig 2

Fig 3

Fig 4

*Right: Victorian saucer showing negative or shallow relief work*

then lean the point slightly over to the right. This allows more of its surface to make contact with the wood. Slowly draw your point across the wood from left to right in a smooth, stroking motion. Don't press into the wood. Try to make a long stroke in order to cover as large an area as you can. The slower you go, the darker the burn will be (Fig 1).

You should now have a broad, even, brown 'band' across the wood. Start a second band, placing your point so that it just touches the bottom edge of your first band. Remember still to lean the point over to the right. The bands should just touch one another, without the join being visible (Fig 2).

It takes practice to know just how slowly to work and where exactly you need to place each band to achieve a nice uniform effect. You can experiment with the temperature control at different settings and also the 'speed' at which you move the point across the surface of the wood. Fig 3 shows darker shading bands made at a slower speed. Fig 4 shows the effect the same technique produces at a lower temperature. It is worth making the effort necessary to master this technique because you will find it so useful.

I shall refer to it as a 'wash' in the projects that follow. Remember all shading should enhance your work, not detract from it! Your design should look better, not worse, after you have shaded it.

# Negative or shallow relief

This method of dealing with large areas of background was much favoured by the Victorians. I have a small wooden jar with a lid and a matching shallow saucer dating from around the turn of the twentieth century. The elderly lady who gave them to me told me that they had been worked by her father using the Vulcan machine mentioned in the Introduction to this book. The whole of the background on both items had been removed by using this technique. It was these two pieces of work which first gave me the idea that

backgrounds could be treated in a different way, and subsequent research uncovered the name of the technique. It is called negative pokerwork, but I prefer to call it shallow relief because the surface of the wood around the design is burned away, so making it stand up slightly proud of the background.

On a piece of prepared plywood and with the temperature setting at 12 o'clock, place the heated nib on the surface. Allow the nib to burn the wood for a split second, just sufficient to give you a neat, nib-shaped burn mark – usually a small oval shape (Fig 5). Lift off the nib and place it exactly next to and

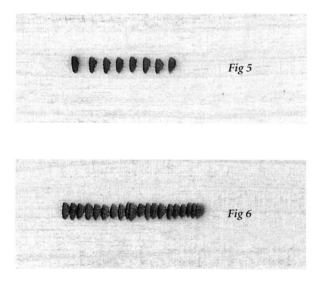

*Fig 5*

*Fig 6*

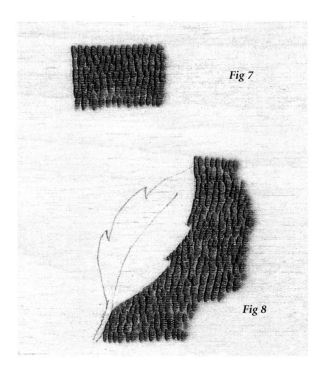

Fig 7

Fig 8

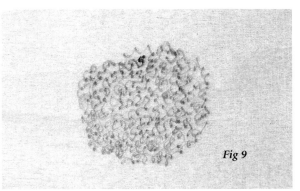

Fig 9

drawn using a double line with a space left between them, as a single burned line would just disappear against the burned background.

# Scribbling, scrolling

Sometimes you will need a background that is light in tone but decorative. This can be achieved by lightly covering the surface with line or what I call 'taking a line for a walk'.

On a piece of prepared plywood, place the heated tip of your point on the surface and 'walk' it over a large area, rather like scribbling, only in a more controlled manner (Fig 9). Aim to produce rounded movements rather than sharp, pointed ones, as these could detract from your design. This kind of background treatment is suitable for use around the main design on such items as boxes, key rings and clocks. Practise these new techniques until you can do them really well.

touching the previous burn. Repeat this about eight or nine times to make a row of burn marks (Fig 6). Then repeat the exercise by placing more burns in rows underneath your first one. Each row should touch the one above. Do sufficient rows to make a decent-sized square (Fig 7).

Now, elsewhere on your wood, draw a simple leaf shape and very carefully burn out the background around the leaf, keeping neat rows where possible (Fig 8). This method, done properly, can be quite time-consuming, as each burn has to be carefully placed, not just performed at random. When using this technique, flower and leaf stems have to be

# PROJECT 3
# VICTORIAN-STYLE BOX
# USING SHALLOW RELIEF

D ecorative pyrographed boxes do not always have to rely upon line and shading techniques. The earlier pyrographers liked to remove the background around their designs so that their work was shown against a darker background. This project mainly uses their techniques to complete a box with an attractive all-over design.

## Tools and materials

Pyrograph with Universal 21 point
Design (from design section)
Veneered sycamore box (125mm/5in square)
HB pencil
Carbon or graphite paper
Tracing paper
Fine sandpaper
Compass
Steel ruler
Masking tape (low tack)
Varnish
Lint-free cloth

## Method

**1**

Sand the box along the grain with the fine sandpaper. Remove the dust with a slightly damp cloth.

**2**

Find the centre of the box lid. To do this, place the ruler diagonally across the lid from corner to corner and lightly draw a pencil line. Repeat for the other two corners. Where these two diagonal lines cross is the centre of the lid. Mark this point (Fig 1).

**3**

Take your compass and set the distance between the two arms to 55mm (2¼in). Place the point of the compass at the centre spot where the two diagonals cross and draw a circle. Reset the distance between the two arms to 50mm (2in), place the point again on the centre spot and draw the smaller circle inside the one already marked (Fig 2).

**4**

Trace your design from the design section (page 75) by placing tracing paper over it and, using a sharp pointed pencil, carefully drawing over the lines. Check that it is all traced before you remove the paper.

**5**

Place a piece of carbon or graphite paper (cut to the size of the design) on the box top. Position the traced design over this and fix it to the box with small pieces of masking tape to keep it in place. Draw carefully over the outlines of the design, and check that everything shows on the wood before you remove it.

**6**

Switch on your machine, setting the heat control at 12 o'clock. When the point is hot enough, draw carefully over the pencilled circles. Keep turning the box to help you get a nice, evenly burned line.

*Fig 1*

*Fig 2*

**7**

Burn carefully over the rest of your design, but only over the outlines. Turn the box to make it easier for you to do this.

# How to do the shallow relief

## Method

**1**

Place your heated point with the tip towards and touching one of the lines of your design (it does not matter where you begin). Leave the point in contact with the surface for a split second or so, until you have a burn mark of the same shape. Lift off the point and repeat the process, placing the tip on the line and next to the mark you have already made. Repeat until you have worked round part of the design. Carry on repeating the technique in rows, where possible, so that the second and each subsequent row touches the one above it. Continue like this until all the background is burned out. Keep it neat.

*N.B.* If your point is new, it may only make a very small burn mark. To make it bigger, try leaning the point over to the right. This should give you a larger burn area. Your older well-worn points are ideal to keep for negative/shallow relief work.

**2**

When the background is completely burned away, check your outlines carefully. If they have become blurred, reshape them by carefully redrawing them. Burn a line down the centre of the leaves in the corners of the box. Using the wash technique already described, work outwards from the centre line towards the outside edge of the leaf. Shade them slightly deeper in the centre, getting paler towards the outside.

**3**

Next, shade the main design elements, the petals and leaves, as illustrated in the photograph of the finished box. When all the shading is complete, draw in the veins on the leaves and the stamens of the flowers.

**4**

To decorate the sides of the box, set the compass arms at 20mm and 23mm (¾in and ⅞in) respectively. Draw the circles and complete the design in the same way as you did for the top. Look carefully at the finished sides, checking that the outlines are clear. If not, then redraw them where necessary.

**5**

Varnish the box, using either silk, matt or gloss according to your own personal taste (see section on 'Finishing off your work' on page 63).

# PROJECT 4
# BOX USING SCROLLING TECHNIQUE

**T**he design is based upon motifs in popular use during the Victorian era. Scrolling has been used to provide a delicate background tone to enhance the corner designs used on the box. The darker areas on the leaf shapes provide a contrast.

## Tools and materials

Pyrograph with Universal 21 point
Design (from design section)
Veneered sycamore box (125mm/5in square)
H or HB pencil
Carbon or graphite paper
Tracing paper
Compass
Steel ruler
Fine sandpaper
Masking tape (low tack)
Varnish
Lint-free cloth

## Method

**1**

Sand the surface of the box, using the fine
sandpaper, and remove the dust with a slightly
damp cloth.

**2**

Find the centre of the box top as described in
Project 3 previously (see Figs 1 and 2). Set the
distance between the compass arms to 35mm
(1⅜in) and, placing the point of the compass in
the centre where these two diagonals cross, draw
a circle.

**3**

Increase the distance between the compass arms
to 40mm (1⅝in) and draw a second circle outside
the first.

**4**

Repeat steps 2 and 3 around the sides of the box,
finding the centre of each side in the same way as
you did for the top. Make the circles 25mm (1in)
and 20mm (¾in) respectively. Draw the circles inside
one another.

**5**

From the outside edge of the box top, measure and
mark 10mm (⅜in) inwards on each side. Join up the
marks to form a 10mm (⅜in) wide margin around
the top. Repeat for the sides.

**6**

Trace the design from the design section
(see page 76).

**7**

Transfer the design to the box top and sides. To do this,
place a piece of carbon or graphite paper on the surface,
shiny side down. Place the traced design over it and
attach both pieces of paper to the surface with small
pieces of masking tape. Using an H pencil, trace over
the design. Check that you have all the detail you need
on the surface of the box before you remove the design.

**8**

Switch on the pyrograph, set the temperature control
at 12 o'clock and allow the machine to warm up.
Outline all of the design with your 21 point. Take
care to make good even lines.

**9**

Starting with the box lid and working from the pointed
edges of the 'leaf' shapes, shade them by stroking the
point across the surface in the direction of the stem
using a wash technique. Repeat on all the leaf shapes.

**10**

Using the tip, scroll the background around the
'leaf' shapes in all the corners. This is done by
drawing the point over the surface in a continuous
scribbling or scrolling type of line, as outlined
earlier in this section. Scroll round the leaf shapes
inside the centre circle.

**11**

Next fill in the large circular band with a solid brown
burn. Drag the point slowly across the surface
between the two outlines. This will produce a darkish

brown area. Be careful not to stray over the outlines. You could of course make a much darker brown burn if you wish, the choice is yours.

you did the top. Try to keep the burn colour of the circular bands, 'leaf' shading and scrolling the same colour as the top.

**12**

Before working on the sides of the box, tape the top of the box to the bottom, carefully matching up any lines of the design that join up. This will stop the lid from moving while you are working on the lines over the join. Complete the sides in the same way as

**13**

Check the design carefully and see if anything needs to be emphasized or tidied up. If you are sure that all is to your satisfaction, then finish off the box by applying two or three coats of varnish to it.

# COLOUR TECHNIQUES

*C*olour can be used in pyrography to enhance the appearance of your work. It is important that colour is not applied thickly so as to block out the delicate linework that you have spent a long time creating. Large areas of burned surface may not take the paint, so if you intend using colour on these, keep your pokerwork to the minimum. It is advisable to complete all the pokerwork first, as this 'seals' the end grains of the wood, preventing the colour from running into areas where you do not want it. There are all kinds of colour media to choose from and it is worth experimenting with these on a piece of plywood until you find one which appeals to you, and suits your ideas and the style of your work. Some you might like to try are:

**Coloured inks including drawing or calligraphy inks**
These can be purchased in a wide range of colours. They can be mixed together to extend the range. You can use them full strength or dilute them with water.

**Wood dyes and wood finishes**  New products are continually being introduced to the market for use on wood – from spirit dyes to water-based coloured wood washes. They are available in a variety of shades, but they can be quite expensive and not easy to find in the small amounts you will use. Spirit-based dyes can be mixed together to increase the range, and they can be diluted by adding white spirit. Do try these out on scrap wood before using them on your work. They can look very different when they

*Selection of pyrographed and painted items*

have dried. Use a small artist's brush and pick up the colour sparingly on the tip of the brush. Spirit dyes evaporate quickly and dry very fast. When applying over large areas you may get a streaky effect.

**Acrylics**  Available in many colours. They are quite thick, but can be thinned with water. They are quick-drying and quite matt in appearance when applied.

**Gouache**  A thick, opaque, cream-like paint when used straight out of the tube. It can be diluted with water. When used undiluted, it will cover all your pokerwork. When water is added, it becomes translucent like pure watercolour.

**Watercolour**  My preferred medium for colouring pyrography. There are so many colours to choose

*Watercolour paints are excellent for applying to wood*  **Fig 1**

from, that you could get carried away selecting the ones that appeal to you. I spend a lot of my time drawing and painting flowers and cannot resist the lovely display of tubes of paint in a good art shop. You do not need lots of different paints, just a few well-chosen colours mixed together will give you all the hues you are likely to use. They can be used as a thinly pigmented wash or as a much stronger-coloured one. To achieve the latter, you need to add much more pigment to a small amount of water. Watercolours are mainly transparent, although a few of them are opaque. They have a luminosity which really brings life to the work when they are applied. Large areas can be covered quite easily – the water sinks into the wood leaving the colour on the surface. It dries quickly and takes varnish well.

**Oil paints** I do not feel these are suitable for use with pyrography: they are opaque and tend to blot out any delicate linework. As they are also oil-based, the paint can sink into the surface of the wood, leaving a greasy stain. They can be diluted with white spirit or special thinners made specifically for this purpose. You may like to try them despite my reservations, but bear in mind that traditional oil paints take a long time to dry.

## Tools and materials

Paints of your choice. If using watercolours, Winsor and Newton Artists' quality are very good. They are a little more expensive than other brands but the quality is excellent. Cheap children's paints are usually not suitable because they nearly always contain white in their mix, giving a cloudy look to the work. Your basic palette (Fig 1) should contain: alizarin crimson, ultramarine blue, vermilion hue, raw umber, cadmium yellow pale, Payne's grey, Chinese white

Plate or tray to mix paints on

Brushes nos. 2 and 4. These should be sufficient for most of your work. If you need larger ones to cover bigger areas, nos. 6 or 8 should be large enough. I use Prolene Pro-Art series 101 brushes. These are inexpensive, have a good point which keeps its shape, and they wear well.

*Fig 2*

## Method for mixing colours

You can increase your range of colours by mixing together combinations of your basic palette. To do this you must carefully control the amount of one colour as you add it to another. Here is an example using ultramarine blue and cadmium yellow pale.

**1**

Make a pool of yellow. Do not make it too thin and make enough to allow you to mix up quite a few different shades of green. Take a little of this paint from the pool and paint a square of yellow.

**2**

Do not clean the brush, pick up a very small amount of blue and mix this into the whole pool of yellow. When fully mixed in, paint a second square next to the yellow one, leaving a little space between the two.

**3**

Repeat step 2 again and again, gradually adding small amounts of blue to the pool of yellow. The yellow should gradually turn green. After each addition of blue, paint a sample square of the new mix (Fig 2).

## Applying colour

The time to add colour is when you are sure that you have completed all the pyrography and before you apply the varnish. Mix the colour you require and add water a little at a time to dilute it into a fairly thin, transparent colour. Using a no. 2 or a no. 4 brush, paint in the chosen area. If the colour looks washed out, add more pigment to your mix and paint over the area again. It is better to start with the paint too thin, as thicker paint will obliterate your design. Whichever medium you choose to colour your work, remember that it should be used to enhance and complement it, not overpower or obscure it.

It is a good idea to experiment with mixing your basic colours together and to keep a record of which colour you added to which. You can note these mixes in a series of sample squares, as shown below (Fig 3).

*Fig 3*

# PROJECT 5
# JEWELLERY BOX USING SHALLOW RELIEF WITH COLOUR

S ometimes you may want to produce a box as a special personal gift. This design enables you to use the oval areas to add in any personal names or messages. The colours of the pansies could be colour co-ordinated with the ribbon.

## Tools and materials

Pyrograph with Universal 21 point
Design (from design section)
Veneered sycamore box (200mm x 120mm x
    80mm/8in x 4¾in x 3in deep)
HB pencil
Tracing paper
Fine sandpaper
Watercolour paints
Artist's brushes nos. 2 and 3
Masking tape (low tack)
Water container
Palette or plate (to mix on)
Varnish

## Method

**1**

Using fine sandpaper, sand the top and sides of the box. Make sure you sand along the grain. Remove the dust with a slightly damp cloth.

**2**

Carefully trace your design from the design section (see page 77).

**3**

Measure and mark out a 5mm (⅛in) border around each side panel and around the box top.

**4**

Cut a piece of carbon or graphite paper to match the size of the top, and place this on top of the box, underneath the traced design. Check that the design falls symmetrically inside the narrow border. Fasten both items down with small pieces of masking tape.

**5**

Using a sharp pencil, gently trace over the design. Check that all the lines have transferred to the box top before you remove the tracing and the carbon paper. Your outline should be visible on the surface of the wood.

**6**

Plug in your pyrograph and set the temperature control at 12 o'clock. When the point is warm, carefully outline the design.

**7**

Burn out the background around the design using the negative/shallow relief technique. Do not burn into the 5mm border; leave this unworked to frame the design. Take extra care when burning out the background around the stems so that you do not 'lose' them. Finally tidy up any raggedy outlines (as described in Project 3).

**8**

Put in the pansy 'faces' (the darker patches around the centre of the flower) (Fig 1). Using the 'wash' method, work the point from the centre outwards (Fig 2). You want to achieve a darker burn which gets paler towards the centre of the petal.

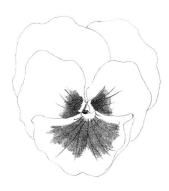

*Fig 1*

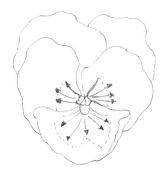

*Fig 2*

*Fig 3*

*Fig 4*

**9**

Using the same technique, lightly shade in the folds in the pansies' petals (Fig 3). Reduce the heat setting on the machine to do this. Starting at the outer edges of the petals, stroke the point towards, but not into, the centre. Be careful to make the shading follow the natural contours of the petal, i.e. the way the petal grows.

**10**

Shade the leaves using the same method, working the nib from the centre vein towards the outer edges. Shade the ribbon folds in the same way (Fig 4).

Now look carefully at your design and check if you have missed any areas, or feel that you have not put in sufficient shading. Remember that you still have to paint the box. Repeat these steps to complete the sides. The oval shape is left unworked. You can insert some initials here.

# Adding colour

You will need your paints, brushes, a water pot and a mixing palette or plate.

## Method

**1**

Begin with the leaves. Using different shades of green, make a thin wash and apply this with care to the leaves and stems. Change the greens a little on each leaf as you paint it. You may want to make the stem a slight browny green.

**2**

Paint the ribbon next. I used ultramarine and white. You may find that the paint will not stay on the shaded areas. In this case I prefer to leave things as they are, because you would need thick paint to cover the area.

Pansies exhibit lovely and unusual colour combinations, even on a single flower. For ideas on colour combinations, look at examples in the garden or, failing that, plant and seed catalogues usually contain excellent photographs. Nearly all pansies have a little white pad at either side of the flower's centre, and usually a little yellow/orange dab below that (Fig 5). When painting, it is possible to blend another colour into one already applied to the surface while it is still wet. If you wish, you can paint the flowers just one colour.

Once all the leaves and flowers have been tinted, you can varnish the box to seal and protect it. Two or three coats of varnish should be sufficient.

*Fig 5*

# PROJECT 6
# KITCHEN CLOCK WITH HERBS

H erbs are always popular as a design source. There is an increasing interest in gardening and the growing of herbs for culinary and medicinal purposes. This clock would make an attractive and appropriate centrepiece in any kitchen.

## Tools and materials

Pyrograph with Universal 21 point
Design (from design section)
Veneered sycamore clock blank
Battery-operated clock movement with hands
HB pencil
Eraser
Steel ruler
Carbon or graphite paper
Watercolour paints
Artist's brushes nos. 2 and 4
Masking tape (low tack)
Water container
Palette or plate (to mix on)
Varnish
Lint-free cloth

## Method

**1**

Prepare the blank by sanding with fine sandpaper along the grain. Remove the dust.

**2**

Trace the design from the pattern provided (see page 78).

**3**

Place a piece of carbon or graphite on the blank and position the traced design over it. Secure both with small pieces of masking tape.

**4**

Using a pencil, trace over the design carefully and check that all of it appears on the wood before removing the carbon and tracing paper.

**5**

Plug in and switch on the pyrograph, with the heat control set at 12 o'clock. When the point is warm enough, outline the design carefully. As this design relies on colour, you may decide to use very little shading, in complete contrast to Project 5. You can apply a little shade to the lavender heads, sage leaf, chives and comfrey leaves. Use the wash method and scrolling for the chive flowerheads.

# Painting the herbs

**Comfrey** (top left) Mix ultramarine with a little yellow to make your green. Using a thin wash, apply the colour carefully to the stems, keeping inside the lines. Mix a little more yellow into your green mix and use this new colour on your leaves. For the flowers, mix a little ultramarine and a little crimson together to make a mauve colour – now add a little white to turn it into a lilac. Apply this to the flowers.

**Rosemary** (top middle) Mix ultramarine with a little yellow to make your green. This time, it needs to be a little on the blue side. Add a little white to this to make it look silvery. Paint this colour inside the leaves. For the stems mix raw umber with a little of your blue, and paint this inside the stems.

**Chives** (top right) You will need your yellow and blue mix for the leaves. The flower heads are a mix of crimson and white, which makes a pale pink colour. You will need raw umber for the chive bulbs; blend a little white into this at the neck of the bulb.

**Dill** (bottom left) A mix of raw umber with a little blue to darken it for the stems bearing the seed heads. For the thicker stems, mix up your green again.

**Lavender** (bottom middle) Mix up the silvery green colour as for the rosemary, only this time add more white to make it really pale silver-green. Paint this in the leaf shapes. For the long petals at the top of the flower, mix up a little crimson, blue and enough white to make a lavender shade. For the bottom part of the flowerhead, add some raw umber to a little crimson and paint it into this part of the flower.

**Sage** (bottom right) The stem and leaves will need a mix of your blue and yellow. The petals are a mix of crimson and white; blend in a little more white on the tips of the large petals. On the cups of the flowers, paint in a mix of raw umber and crimson.

# How to mark a clock face

You may want to change the size of a clock face, or place it in a different position, when you prepare another clock. You may find the following method helps you.

## Tools

Compass
HB pencil
Steel ruler
Eraser
Protractor

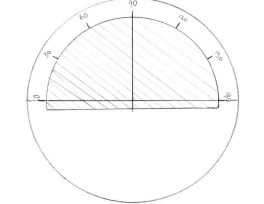

*Fig 1*

## Method

**1**

Use the compass to draw a circle the size that you want the clock face to be.

**2**

Using the ruler, draw a line horizontally through the exact centre point of the circle. It must be level (Fig 1).

**3**

Take the protractor and lay the straight edge exactly on the horizontal line. Line up the vertical centre line on the protractor, so that it sits exactly on the centre point of the circle.

*Fig 2*

**4**

Now mark off the hours as follows. Working to the left of the protractor's centre line, place a pencil mark at the 0, 30, 60 and 90 degree measurements. Then, working to the right of the centre, mark at 120, 150 and 180 degrees. The top half of the clock is now marked with the positions of the hours (Fig 2). Place the protractor over the bottom half with the straight edge on the centre line (as for the top) and repeat so that the hours are also marked off on the bottom section of the clock face (Fig 3). You must be accurate.

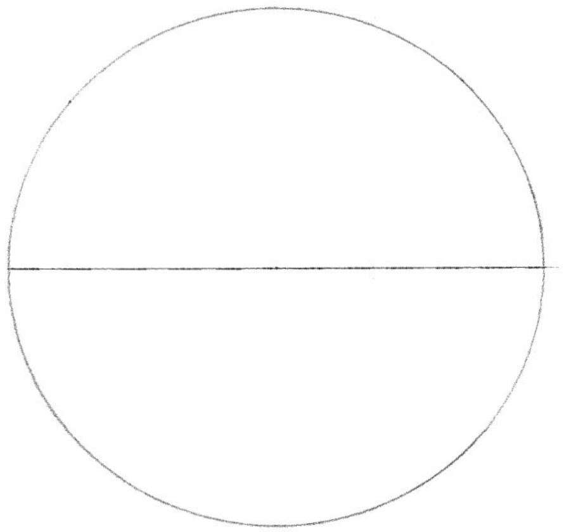

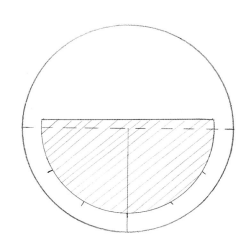

*Fig 3*

# FUR AND FEATHER TECHNIQUES

**H**aving worked through the earlier projects, you should now be familiar with your machine and quite adept at manipulating the point to produce the line and tone work that you want. This chapter combines some of the previous techniques, and explains how to apply them in a more advanced way to produce the effect of fur and feathers.

It is important to select the most suitable combination to capture the look of the subject you are working on, and this needs careful thought before you begin burning. When you have decided on your subject, study it carefully and try to see it as a series of different lines and areas of tone. Then think which technique would best help you to achieve the finish that will most closely resemble your chosen subject. Combinations of techniques will vary from subject to subject. Look closely at the fur and feathers you wish to portray. How best can you show the nature of fur, for example. Ask yourself: 'Is it short, long, curly, wavy, straight or smooth?' 'In which direction does it lie over the different areas of the animal's body?' 'Will short straight lines, curved ones or broken ones depict it best?' Try a test piece first!

When drawing any animal or bird, pay particular attention to the eye. Its size, shape and position in the head needs to be as accurately observed and placed as you can manage. I feel it is better for the eye to be slightly larger than it is in life, rather than smaller. Above all, do not forget to give it a lively sparkle by adding the highlight to the pupil (by means of an area of unburned or lightly burned wood). Without it, the subject will look dead.

When you choose your wildlife subject, make sure that you have good reference material available to study. This should clearly show you its particular features. Take a mouse, for example. There are different kinds of mice; all look similar, but certain features distinguish them from each other – from the tiny, delicate harvest mouse to the cheeky, large-eared, large-eyed wood mouse, or the sleepy-looking, chubby dormouse. These distinguishing features should be accurately recorded in your work, so that other people will be able to recognize clearly which species you have illustrated.

The techniques you will employ for the next few projects will be drawn from pages 7–9 and 21–3; line-hatching, wash and scrolling. You can, of course, look at those other surface finishes you created on your sampler at the beginning of this book. You may find a pattern that you feel will suit your subject far better than the ones I have suggested. Whichever you decide to use, you may find it safer to work lightly initially, as mistakes are easier to erase. You can darken and emphasize your work where needed at a later stage.

# Fur technique

## Tools and materials

Piece of scrap plywood (sanded down)
Pyrograph with Universal 21 point

## Exercise 1

Using the wash method, cover an area of the scrap plywood, approximately 50mm (2in) square. Try to get the effect nice and even, with no stripes showing. Remember to lean the point over to the right to produce a broader band of wash. You may find that some darker marks appear as you work over the grain.

## Exercise 2

Using a short, sharp line, begin at the top of the square, and cover the shaded area with fine 'hairs' (Fig 1). To produce the hairs, keep the point vertical and, placing the nib on the wood, flick it quickly in a downward movement pulling the point towards you. This should leave short lines. Vary their length and also the place where you start each one, so that they do not look too regular, as if they are in regimental rows.

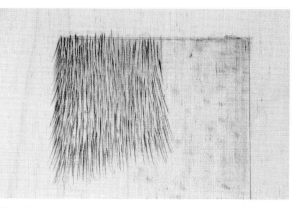

*Fig 1*

## Exercise 3

Trace off the outline of the harvest mouse from the design section (see page 80), and transfer this onto your practice piece. Using the wash technique, fill in the body of the mouse with it, beginning at the nose and pulling the bands of wash down towards the tail. Do not outline the shape of the mouse with a solid line. Now draw the fine lines for the fur (Fig 2). Begin at the nose and work down towards the tail. Pull the point towards the nose, not from the nose towards the tail. You can extend these fur lines over the edge of the 'wash' to break up the outline of the mouse. Make sure the lines follow the natural curve and bend of the body. When you reach the tail, again break the outline over the point where the tail joins the body.

*Fig 2*

## Exercise 4 – harvest mouse eye

First of all, draw an enlarged eye as this is easier to work with than a small one, and allows you to appreciate the shading and line control required when you come to work on the smaller eye in the design.

Outline the eye using the 21 point. Draw over the outer line first, keeping the line as fine as possible. To make a fine line, it helps to keep the point in an upright position. Now draw over the inner line. Fill in the pupil of the eye by scrolling over the surface to produce a dark, smooth, even tone. Remember to leave the highlight! Softly shade the lighter rim around the pupil (Fig 3).

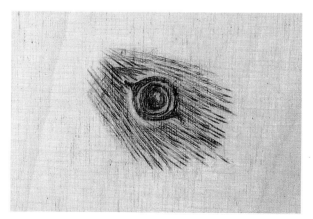

*Fig 3*

# PROJECT 7
# HARVEST MOUSE WITH POPPIES

T he harvest mouse provides a nice uncomplicated shape for applying the fur techniques. You may wish to use a different one. If you do, make sure you use it in an appropriate setting, for example, a wood mouse on a branch of blackberries.

## Tools and materials

Pyrograph with Universal 21 point
Design (from design section)
Veneered sycamore panel or birch ply (220mm x
    300mm/8½in x 12in)
H or HB pencil
Carbon or graphite paper
Tracing paper
Eraser
Fine sandpaper
Masking tape (low tack)
Varnish
Lint-free cloth

## Method

**1**

Prepare the panel by sanding it carefully along the grain until you have a very smooth surface. Wipe off the dust.

**2**

Trace off the design from the design section (see page 80), using a broken line to indicate the outline of the mouse.

**3**

Transfer the traced design onto the prepared panel. Remember to fix the graphite paper and tracing paper onto the wood with small pieces of masking tape, before you begin tracing the design. Check that you have transferred all the information you need before removing the traced design and graphite paper.

**4**

Warm up the pyrograph and, with the heat control set at 12 o'clock, carefully outline your traced drawing, leaving the outline of the mouse unworked. Keep the lines as fine as possible and do not press the point into the surface, but let it glide across the wood. Aim for a burn line that is not too dark. You can always go over it at the end if you feel that it is not dark enough.

**5**

Beginning with the wheat, and using the wash technique, work on each individual seed, making the base of each one deeper in tone than the rest of the seed. Now burn a line from the point of each seed to about halfway down its length. 'Wash' down the stem making it a darker tone underneath the tail and feet of the mouse. Now flick in the 'hairs' around the ear of the wheat (Fig 1).

**6**

Apply a wash to the grass stems, again burning a darker tone where the blade of grass crosses the stem and also where it folds back on itself. Wherever the stem disappears behind or beneath another part of the design, shade this area darker as suggested on the design. Carefully draw in the fine lines (grooves) down the stem and the vein lines along the blade of grass (Fig 2).

*Fig 1*

*Fig 2*

*Fig 3*  *Fig 4*  *Fig 5*

**7**

For the poppy petals, slightly lower the heat so that when you apply the wash to the folds in the petals, they will look delicate and not too heavy. To shade the petal folds, gently stroke the point from the outer edge of the petal towards the centre of the flower. Ease the point off the surface so that only a small area has a brown tone on it (Fig 3). Avoid making the petals look as if they have stripes!

**8**

Turn up the heat again and burn in the darker patches in the centre of the petals.

**9**

For the poppy with few petals, carefully shade from underneath the 'lid' of the seed case down to the base, leaving a band of shading. Repeat this effect around the seed case, leaving a narrow unburned section between each band (as in Fig 3). For the pollen stalks around the base of the seed case, burn in a few curved lines, varying their length. Finish off the top of these by placing just the tip of the point on the top of the line and burning a dot.

**10**

Now shade in the poppy stems and carefully flick in tiny lines to represent the hairs that grow on the stems. Do the same for the casing of the poppy bud (Fig 4).

**11**

To work the daisy petals, reduce the heat and carefully stroke each petal to leave a faint striped effect. Where one petal crosses another, shade the underneath petal darker at the point where the two cross (Fig 5).

**12**

For the daisy centres, shade up one side and a little around the base to suggest the pollen heads. Scroll over the shading to give a rougher surface texture. You may need to increase the heat for this or scroll more slowly.

**13**

Shade in the poppy leaves, working from the centre vein out towards the edge, with the darker area in the centre getting lighter towards the outside edge.

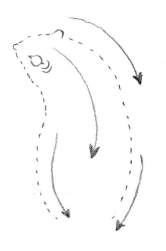

*Fig 6*

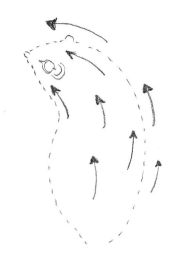

*Fig 7*

**14**

Using the wash technique, fill in the body of the mouse, beginning at the nose and pulling the bands of wash down towards the tail (Fig 6).

**15**

Now draw the fine lines for the fur. Begin at the nose and work down towards the tail. Pull the point towards the nose, not from the nose towards the tail (Fig 7). You can extend these fur lines over the edge of the 'wash' to break up the outline of the mouse. Make sure the lines follow the natural curve and bend of the body. When you reach the tail,

again break the outline over the point where the tail joins the body.

**16**

See exercise 4 page 40 for how to draw the mouse's eye.

**17**

Check your work and make any alterations to the tone and line at this stage. Finish off the project by applying one to three coats of clear varnish (gloss or satin according to the type of finish you prefer). Use a lint-free cloth to apply it. Make sure it is completely dry before applying subsequent coats.

# PROJECT 8
# KITTEN'S HEAD

T he fluffiness of a kitten's fur is an ideal subject for pyrography, allowing you to use a combination of wash and line techniques. Though a more difficult project than the mouse, the end result will be worth the effort.

## Tools and materials

Pyrograph with Universal 21 point
Design (from design section)
Plywood blank or plaque (165mm x 210mm/6½in
    x 8¼in)
HB pencil
Carbon or graphite paper
Tracing paper
Fine sandpaper
Masking tape (low tack)
Varnish
Lint-free cloth

*Fig 1*

Pupil with highlight

Iris - coloured part of the eye

## Method

**1**

Prepare the panel by sanding it with the fine
sandpaper, along the grain. Check that the surface
feels smooth to the touch, then remove any dust.

**2**

Trace off the design from the design section (see
page 81) and transfer it to the prepared panel, as
outlined in previous projects. Do not use a solid line
for the outline of the head and body; use a broken
one. Check that you have transcribed all the details
you need before you remove the tracing and
graphite paper.

**3**

Warm up the pyrograph with the heat setting at
12 o'clock. For this project you will have to keep
varying the heat to produce the soft tones needed
for the kitten.

**4**

Beginning with the eyes, outline the very outer edge
first, keeping the line dark and very fine. Carefully
stroke the point (using the wash technique) from the
inner corner of the eye along the bottom of the iris
(the coloured part of the eye), making a light brown
wash. Burn in the pupil, remembering to leave the
highlight unburned (Fig 1).

*Fig 2*

**5**

Using the scrolling technique, scroll over the iris,
making it slightly darker in tone near the inner
corner of the iris. The highlight can be emphasized
by scratching over it with a sharp pointed blade to
increase the contrast (Fig 2).

**6**

Work the end of the nose using the stipple technique
for the outline and for the centre line of the nose and
upper lip (Fig 3).

*Fig 3*

*Fig 4*

*Fig 5*

**7**

Working from the top edge of the nose, stroke a wash upward towards the top of the head and between the ears. As you move up the head, fan the lines out to the left and right in the direction of the growth of the fur (Fig 4). Keep the wash light all over at this stage.

**8**

Now deepen the wash inside the ears, working from the tip downwards. Now deepen the tone behind the ears (Fig 5).

**9**

Reduce the heat and using the wash, take your time and fill in a light base tone all over the head area, trying to keep the 'bands' as even as possible. Fade the wash away as you move to the outer edges of the head and ears. Remember to keep everything light at this stage.

**10**

Using small strokes placed close together, work on the tip of the nose to give it a little more texture.

**11**

For the 'tabby' bands, use a zigzag stroke (Fig 6), referring to the photograph of the finished panel on page 45 for their position. Alternatively you can copy the pattern of a cat's markings from a photograph.

*Fig 6*

The zigzag stroke is achieved by moving the point up and down, keeping the lines close together, and varying the lengths of the 'zigzags'. This helps to imitate the varying thicknesses of the tabby markings. For darker bands, go slowly – you may also have to increase the heat above the 12 o'clock setting. For the lighter bands, move over the surface more quickly and reduce the heat. You may wish to practise this technique before you attempt to use it on the head. The zigzag will form the basis for the fine hairs, which will be superimposed over the bands once all the tabby markings are in place. If the lines in the bands show a little too much, shade over them with a wash and this will help to blend them together. Keep working over the whole head, blending in the bands and gradually increasing the tones around the mouth and chin.

12

Once all the tabby bands are completed and you have established the overall tones as you want them, you can begin to put in the individual hairs where appropriate. They do not need to cover the whole head. Place them where they will help to show the growth direction of the fur. You can also use them to break up the outline of the head and ears.

13

Scratch in the whiskers where they extend over the dark tones and, using a hot nib, draw them in where they go over the light tones.

14

Check your work and, if you are happy with it, then complete it by applying the finish of your choice.

# Feather technique

Feathers on birds vary in their appearance, texture and relative size around the body. The plumage on the head, breast, underbody and the area between the wings is usually soft and quite small in proportion to the size of the bird. Wing and tail feathers are usually stiffer and have a pronounced central shaft to give them the rigidity needed to support the bird in flight. Many birds have distinctive markings, which look like bands, on their feathers. They may vary in size up the length of one feather, or the feather may have just a dark tip. Careful observation is necessary. When working feathers in pyrography, you will have to select the techniques which will enable you accurately to represent the appearance of the bird you are depicting. You may find that you have to combine different techniques as you did for the previous project.

## Tools and materials

Pyrograph with Universal 21 point
Piece of prepared plywood
Photographs of birds for reference

## Exercise 1

Using a photograph as reference, draw the breast area of a bird on your piece of plywood. Cover this with a wash effect, setting the temperature control at 12 o'clock. Keeping the tone light, work from under the beak down towards the underbelly and leg area. Do not draw a hard outline as you would not see this in real life. Try to keep the wash smooth and even. You may find that you pick up a few of the end grains, which will give you a darker area, as you work across. Sometimes this can add to the effect. Add another wash underneath the wing to give it a darker tone. If you need to, blend this into the chest by doing a wash over the whole area.

## Exercise 2

Draw the centre line of a feather, then beginning at the top and stroking away from the centre to the outer edge of the feather, work down it using the wash method. Keeping the wash lines diagonal, work around the bottom edge of the centre line. Now work down the other side again starting from the top (Fig 1).

*Fig 1*

*Fig 2*  *Fig 3*  *Fig 4*

## Exercise 3

Now work another wash across the bottom of the feather to make a dark tip on the feather's edge (Fig 2).

## Exercise 4

Add some very fine lines, beginning at the centre line at the top of the feather. Pull these lines diagonally out and slightly downwards, towards the outer edge where they can extend slightly over the edge of the wash (Fig 3).

## Exercise 5

Repeat exercises 2 and 3 on another feather. Now using a zigzag stroke, reduce the heat and add a band of darker marking across the feather (Fig 4). Darken the tip, then add fine lines. Cover with a soft wash. If the feathers need to be light ones, then reduce the heat for these steps. Use your reference material for the feather patterns.

## Exercise 6 – overlapping feathers

Using a reduced heat setting, draw in the centre lines of two feathers about 13mm (½in) apart. Apply a wash to both of them working from the centre line outwards, as in the previous exercises. The washes should meet in the middle between the two. Where the two edges meet, draw in another centre line downward to make a third feather (Fig 5). Darken the area underneath the two upper ones. Avoid getting a hard edge around the tips of these. Using the wash,

*Fig 5*

*Fig 6*

work this third feather as you did the other two. Add any feather bars, using the zigzag technique, on the upper ones. Now draw in the fine lines diagonally and downwards from the centre line to the outside edge of each one.

## Exercise 7

For the softer, less rigid feathers which overlap tail and wing feathers, use a soft wash and, working from the tip, stroke the surface to make a feather shape. Fade the wash out as you move up the feather. Add a faint centre line (Fig 6). Now add very faint lines using a reduced heat setting.

## Exercise 8

Tail feathers are worked like wing feathers except that they can be much longer. Work them as in exercises 2–5. You may find areas of a slightly darker tone at regular intervals along the length of the tail feather. To achieve this, add a second wash over any areas where it is required (Fig 7).

*Fig 7*

# PROJECT 9
# WREN ON CONVOLVULUS

T*he wren is a very shy, tiny bird, always popular as an image on greetings cards. This project combines the simple shape of the wren with the more* *flambuoyant shapes of the convolulus. You will need to combine quite a few of your accquired techniques to capture the fragility of the wren.*

## Tools and materials

Pyrograph with Universal 21 point
Design (from design section)
Piece of birch ply (220mm x 300mm/8½in x 12in)
HB pencil
Eraser
Carbon or graphite paper
Tracing paper
Very fine sandpaper
Masking tape (low tack)
Watercolours
Artist's brushes nos. 2 and 4
Mixing plate or palette
Water pot
Varnish
Lint-free cloth

## Method

**1**

Using a sharp pencil, trace the design from the design section (see page 82). Draw carefully over the outlines and details such as eyes.

**2**

Prepare the birch panel by sanding it along the grain with the sandpaper. Make sure the surface is very smooth. Remove the dust.

**3**

Transfer the tracing-paper design onto the wood by placing it over the graphite paper and attaching both pieces of paper to the panel with small pieces of masking tape.

**4**

Carefully trace over the outlines, keeping to the outer edge of the lines and using a sharp pencil. Check that you have recorded all the information you need before you remove the tracing and graphite paper.

**5**

Warm up the pyrograph with the heat setting at 12 o'clock. Carefully outline the design, but do not use a solid line for the wren's chest, leave this unworked at this stage (Fig 1).

**6**

Beginning with the branches, and using a curved shading stroke, work from left to right across the branch. Ease off the point as you get about half to two-thirds of the way across. This will produce an area of darker shading down the left-hand side of all the branches. Where leaves or stems cross the branches, use areas of darker shading where the two elements meet (Fig 2). You can add sharper, curved lines in places on the branches to give them more character. If you leave some areas of unburned wood between these curved lines, it helps to suggest the roughness of the bark.

*Fig 1*

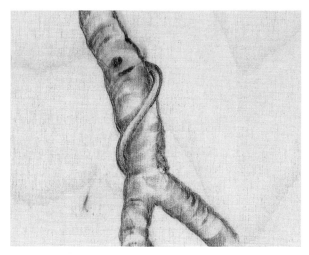

*Fig 2*

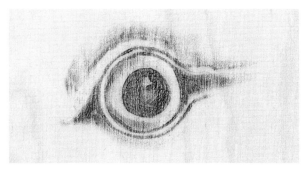

*Fig 3*

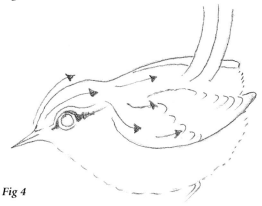

*Fig 4*

*Fig 5*

## Method to work the wren

**1**

Using as fine a line as you can achieve, begin at the point of the beak and draw along the top of the head and down the back. Draw a line on either side of the tail and a very fine line down the centre of it.

**2**

Burn a line along the bottom edge of the wing.

**3**

Outline the underside of the beak but do not draw the outline of the bird's breast – leave this until a later stage.

**4**

To work the eye, draw round the pupil, then draw a smaller circle inside this (as you did for the mouse). Fill in this smaller circle with a nice, dark, even burn, but leave a small white dot for the highlight. This brings the eye to life. Burn a short line from the outside corner of the eye towards the back of the bird's head. Leaving a small space beneath the eye, gently draw in a line around the bottom of the eye (Fig 3).

**5**

Using the wash method, and working from the back edge of the beak, softly shade the upper half of the head following its curve. Carry this wash shading along the upper body to the tail. Shade the shoulder section of the wing (Fig 4). This should lay a soft brown tone on these areas over which you may work the feathers.

**6**

Using a soft wash, shade the wren's chest, starting under the beak and working towards the tail. Work a darker area under the wing (Fig 5).

**7**

Shade in the tail using a light tone, then, with a darker tone, burn in the bands across the tail using a short line-stroke. Reduce the heat and use the same technique to make smaller, fainter bars on the wren's chest (Fig 6).

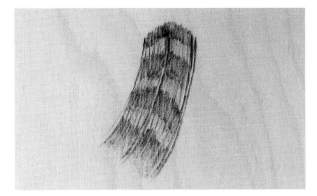

*Fig 6*

*Fig 7*

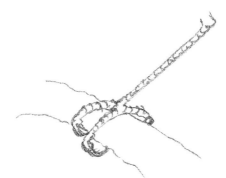

*Fig 8*

**8**

Using very short fine strokes and starting beneath the tail, work towards the front of the bird's breast, drawing these fine lines all over the chest area and ensuring that they get paler towards the beak.

**9**

On the wing, the outline of the main feathers can be burned in and extra shading added. Draw the long line of the feathers along the wing edge. Burn in the wing bars (Fig 7).

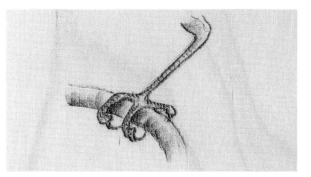

*Fig 9*

**10**

Using a very fine line, draw in the outline of the legs and the claws (Fig 8). Keep the legs very thin, as the wren is a tiny delicate bird. Draw in the fine markings on the legs (Fig 9).

## Method for the convolvulus and leaves

**1**

Check that all the leaves are outlined and draw in the centre vein. Delineate the side veins in a lighter tone.

**2**

Work on each section of the leaf, one at a time. Starting from the central vein, stroke out towards the outer edge. Start with a darker tone in the centre by working slowly, then speed up as you get about one-third of the way across, fading out the shading. Carefully shade in the space between two side veins, leaving a narrow unburned line along the vein (Fig 10). If you are unsure how the appearance of

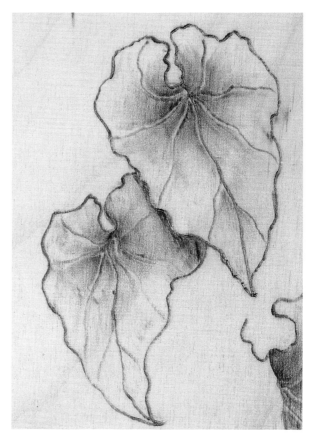

*Fig 10*

a leaf looks, check in a gardening reference book. When all the main shading is completed on the leaves, you can draw in some of the very fine veins on some of them (Fig 11). Do not do this on all the leaves, however, or else the finished work will look too fussy.

**3**

Work on the ivy in the same way.

## Method for the flowers

**1**

Gently outline the flower heads using a reduced heat setting so that the burned outline has a more delicate appearance.

**2**

Still using a low heat, gently shade in the petals around the stamens in the centre. Start dark and fade the tone out as you near the middle of the petal. Gently shade in any folds in the petal as you did on the pansy box.

**3**

Outline the stamens and deepen the tone around them if necessary. Shade from under the bottom edge of the petals down towards the calyx (Fig 12).

**4**

If you have not already done so, outline the calyx and the stem; put in the centre lines and shade upwards from the bottom of the calyx towards the points (Fig 12).

**5**

Once you have worked all the flowers and leaves, look closely at the work, especially where leaves overlap one another or a branch. Check the shadow where this occurs and make sure that you have made it dark enough. If you are satisfied, you can either leave the piece as it is and varnish it, or add a hint of watercolour to the flowers and the leaves before you apply any finish. If you decide to add colour, remember that the flowers are white with a hint of yellow in the centre fading out towards the top. The leaves are green.

*Fig 11*

*Fig 12*

# PROJECT 10
# TAWNY OWL

T his tawny owl is a real test for all the skills you have mastered doing the other projects. By now your skill at line and wash should be good enough to attempt this ambitious project.

## Tools and materials

Pyrograph with Universal 21 point
Design (from design section)
Birch ply panel (225mm x 300mm/9in x 12in)
H or HB pencil
Carbon or graphite paper
Tracing paper
Fine sandpaper
Masking tape (low tack)
Varnish (matt, silk or gloss)
Lint-free cloth

# Method

**1**

Prepare the panel by carefully sanding along the grain until the surface feels very smooth to the touch. Remove any dust.

**2**

Trace the design carefully (see page 83) using a sharp pencil.

**3**

Transfer the design onto the panel by first placing the graphite paper, shiny side down, on the prepared surface. Lay the traced design over it. Attach both pieces of paper to the panel using small strips of masking tape.

**4**

Draw over the traced design putting in all the details you need. Use a sharp pencil to do this and keep to the outside edge of the lines. Before removing the tracing and the graphite paper, check that you have transferred all the details you need. Remove the tracing and graphite paper.

**5**

Warm up the pyrograph with the heat setting at 12 o' clock.

**6**

Starting with the eyes, draw round the outline of the iris and, using the wash technique, stroke over the eyeball leaving the highlight unworked. Use a light tone at this stage.

**7**

Darken the eyeball, leaving the lighter tone showing around the outside edge of the eyeball (Fig 1). Carefully draw in the other fine lines around the eye. Burn in the dark areas immediately around the eye.

**8**

Reduce the heat slightly and, working outwards from the eye towards the large outer circles of the 'spectacle' area, gently stroke the point over the wood using a slightly curved band of a lighter wash tone. Watch the direction of this curve as you move around the eye area, as it will vary in direction (Fig 2).

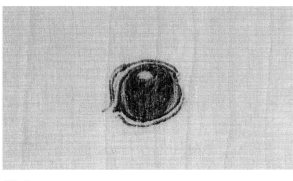

*Fig 1*

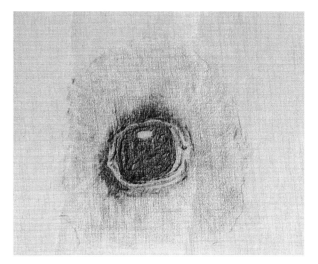

*Fig 2*

**9**

Using a small circular scrolling movement, deepen the tone along the outside edge of the large circles (see finished work on page 56), and down the centre line between the eyes and above the beak.

**10**

Leaving unworked a narrow band all around this dark edge, put a light wash over the rest of the head, working from the side of the eyes outwards. Work in any extra areas of shading. Using small fine strokes, establish the textured area around the bottom of the beak.

**11**

Shade in the beak and the nostrils using fine lines.

**12**

Work over the top and sides of the head, gradually building up the darker areas by gently stroking the point over the surface until you are happy with how it looks.

**13**

Working down the chest from underneath the lower edge of the eye area, stroke in a light tone using the wash technique with a curved stroke. If the wash appears uneven at this stage, do not worry, as we will be working the feathers over the top of this basic wash. Work the back of the owl in the same way down to the first line of the wing feathers.

***Fig 3***

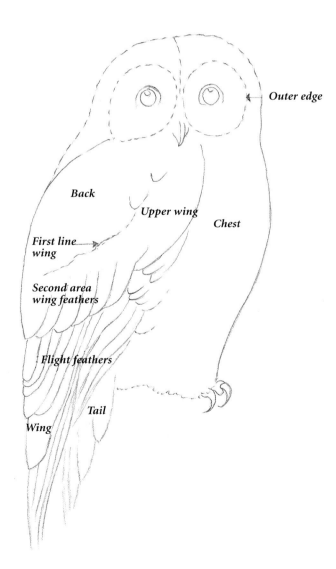

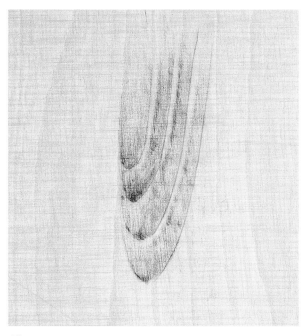

*Fig 4*

*Fig 5*

## Method for the feathers

**1**

Work the area between the first and second line of wing feathers (see the guide to the sections of the owl – Fig 3) by applying a wash in a light tone.

**2**

The wing feathers will need to be worked following the instructions for the flight feathers given below, leaving small bands of unworked wood around the edges of each feather.

**3**

For the flight feathers immediately below the edge of the wing use the wash method and, working from this bottom edge, work each flight feather by pulling the point down towards the tip and fading it out as you near the bottom. Repeat for each feather, but leave a white (unworked) edge between each one of them (Fig 4).

**4**

Where the white edge touches the next feather, darken the area immediately underneath (Fig 5).

**5**

Put in the dark bands on the flight feathers (see finished work) by turning up the heat slightly and using either the zigzag technique employed in Project 8 or lines placed close together. Note that the shape and size of these bands will vary along the feather's length.

**6**

Work the larger, longer flight feathers in the same way.

**7**

Put in the tail using a light tone and employing the wash method. Draw in very fine lines over the top of the feathers, pulling these from the tip towards the middle of each one.

**8**

Put in the markings on the upper wing and back.

**9**

The chest feathers need to be kept light in tone, with slight variations as they curve around the body to suggest its shape, and to give form to the bird. The techniques to use are wash, scrolling, zigzag and fine lines, where appropriate. Keep the heat slightly reduced for this area. When all the shading is complete, then put in the markings.

**10**

Outline the branch and the main features of it.

**11**

Shade the area immediately underneath the owl where it sits on the branch, using a very dark burn. You can turn up the heat control or pull the point more slowly over the surface to achieve this. Now, using a curved stroke, work from the perimeter of the 'hole' in the branch (Fig 6) towards its outer edge. Repeat for the area underneath the 'hole'. Blend the shading together by stroking the point along the branch instead of across it as you have in the previous steps.

**12**

Once all the branch has been shaded in, use scrolling, line and zigzag to establish the pattern of the bark.

**13**

Using a new unused point (if you have one), draw in the thin lines on the long flight feathers as close together and as finely as you can. Treat the very bottom edge of the chest feathers where they rest over the branch in the same way.

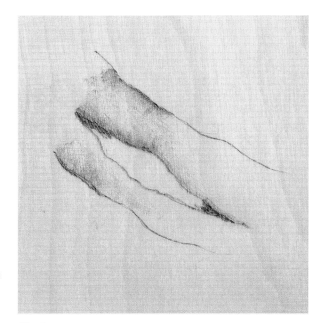

*Fig 6*

**14**

Using a piece of very fine sandpaper and a sharp knife, highlight parts of the larger eye circle by scratching out some of the shading or sanding some of it off.

**15**

Finish off the panel by applying one or more protective coats of varnish and polish. Remember to keep worked pieces out of direct sunlight as this will cause the delicate lines and tones to fade very quickly.

# LEARNING OTHER SKILLS

## Making your own carbon paper

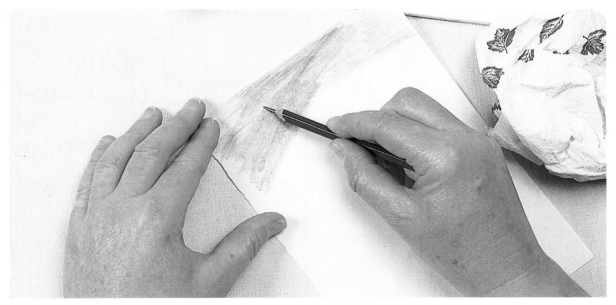

*Fig 1*

### Tools and materials

Sheet of A4 layout paper (available from art or
stationery shops)
HB or B pencil
Soft tissues

### Method

**1**

Carefully place the sheet of layout paper on your
drawing board or desk. Be careful as you handle it
as it is quite thin.

**2**

Incline the point of the lead and then cover the whole
surface of the paper with pencil (Fig 1). Direct the
pencil strokes one way, then another, until the whole
sheet has a dense coating of lead. There should be no
white paper left showing.

**3**

When the paper is adequately coated, polish off the
graphite dust with the tissues. Your carbon paper is
now ready to use.

# Tracing the designs

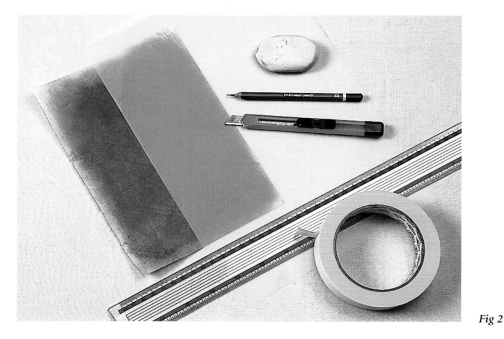

*Fig 2*

## Tools and materials

Tracing paper (A4-size or larger)
H or HB pencil
Ruler
Eraser
Masking tape (low tack)
Pencil sharpener (or sharp knife)
Black carbon paper (or home-made
graphite paper)

## Method

**1**

Place tracing paper over your chosen design. To make sure it does not slip, use small pieces of masking tape to hold it in place.

**2**

With a sharp pencil, carefully draw over the design, keeping to the outer edge of the lines (Fig 2). Put in all details you think you will need, such as eyes, leaf veins, feathers and so on.

**3**

Check that you have traced everything you need before removing the tracing paper. To make sure that you have not missed any part of the design, carefully remove one or two pieces of masking tape and ease up a corner of the tracing paper so that you can look underneath to check the original.

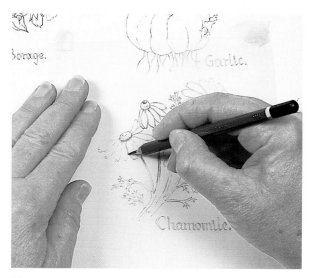

*Fig 2*

# Finishing off the work

*Fig 3*

## Tools and materials

Varnish (gloss or satin)
Lint-free cloth
White spirit (for thinning if necessary)
Stick (for stirring varnish)

It pays to finish off your work with two or three coats of satin or gloss varnish, depending on the finish you prefer. Applying a protective coat keeps your work clean and helps to make it more durable; it enhances the work, especially if it has been coloured. I prefer to apply the varnish with a lint-free cloth rather than a brush (Fig 3). Brushes have a habit of losing hairs, and leaving unsightly brush marks. There is also a tendency to apply varnish too thickly when using a brush. Pyrographed items should always be kept out of direct sunlight, as exposure to sunlight will cause the image to fade over time, especially the most delicate parts of the work.

## Method

**1**

To apply varnish with a cloth, stir it thoroughly and, if it is a little thick, add a few drops of white spirit to thin it. Then stir again.

**2**

Make a small pad of lint-free cloth and lightly dip it into the varnish. Wipe off any surplus on the lip of the tin.

**3**

Apply to the wood with nice even strokes, covering the whole surface (Fig 3). Let it dry overnight, or according to the maker's instructions, before applying subsequent coats. How many coats you apply, depends on how shiny you want the finished article to be.

**4**

Before applying more coats, you will need to sand the varnish coat already applied. To do this, either use very fine wire wool or very fine wet-and-dry sandpaper. Lightly sand the first coat, wipe the surface with white spirit to remove any dust, then apply another coat of varnish. Repeat the process until you have built up as many coats as you wish.

**5**

After your final coat is completely dry, you can finish the job by applying a little furniture polish and buffing it with a soft cloth.

# Lining a box

## Tools and materials

PVA glue
Mounting board (or similar – it needs to be relatively thick)
Velvet (to cover the card)
Pencil
Scissors
Steel ruler
Craft knife

*A box fully lined with velvet*

## Useful tips

- Always use glue sparingly.
- Don't try to cut through thick card in one go. Make several shallow cuts, so that you gradually slice through the whole thickness.
- Line the box after all the external finishing work has been completed.

## Method

**1**

Take the internal measurements of each side of the box. Draw these on the card and then cut out the different pieces using the ruler and the craft knife. Remember to cut the sides fractionally smaller all around to allow for the slight thickness of the material that will overlap the edges.

**2**

Place each piece of card on the fabric, allowing a margin of extra fabric of up to 25mm (1in) around each piece (Fig 1). Cut out each piece of fabric including this overlap.

**3**

Smear a small amount of glue over the whole of one side of a piece of card. Allow the glue to go a little tacky.

*Fig 1*

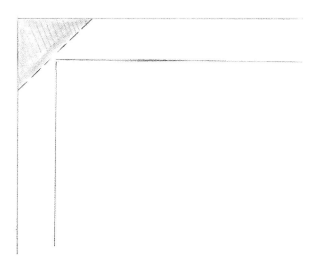

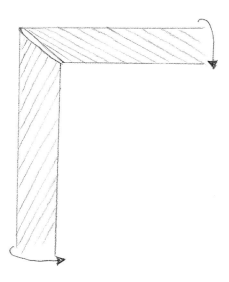

*Fig 2*

*Fig 3*

**4**

Place the card (sticky side down) on the back and in the centre of its fabric and press it down to make sure it is securely attached. Repeat for all the pieces.

At this point you have a choice of how you cope with the corners! Either:

**5**

Cut off the fabric at an angle diagonally across and nearly touching the corner of the card (Fig 2). Smear a small amount of glue on the edges of the uncovered

card in the areas where the fabric will overlap it. Allow the glue to go tacky. Fold the fabric carefully and firmly over each side, so that the cut edges nearly touch one another, and press it firmly onto the back of the card (Fig 3). Allow to dry (Fig 4).

**6**

The other option is to leave the fabric as it is, and glue down two adjoining sides. To do this, smear a small amount of glue onto the edges of the card where the fabric will overlap. Take one side and fold the fabric

*Fig 4*

*Fig 5*

carefully and firmly over the edge of the card and press it onto the back. Repeat with the other side. Where the two sides meet at the corner, pinch both sides of the fabric towards each other so that they meet in a diagonal fold. This will leave a piece of spare fabric sticking up (Fig 5). When the glue is dry, trim off this excess fabric with your scissors as close to the surface of the card as possible. Cover all the pieces of card with fabric in the same way.

**7**

Looking at the back of each piece of card, you will see that an area remains uncovered. If you were to glue it into the box like this, the uncovered area would leave a depression, especially if you are using a thick fabric. To avoid this, cut a piece of fabric to fit this area, and glue it in place on each piece of card.

**8**

Beginning with the base, smear either the bottom of the box, or the back of the card, with a small amount of glue. Allow it to go tacky. Place the card base inside the box and press it down firmly into position. Allow it to dry.

**9**

Secure all the sides in the same manner, gluing the pieces as you use them. When positioning the side pieces, it is a good idea to work on opposite sides together, i.e. the two long sides, then the two short sides. Press the sides down firmly onto the base, which is already in place, to check the fit. Before gluing in the sides, try one side first and check that, when it is in position, it does not stick up above the edge of the box. If it does, lift up the top edge of the fabric on each piece of card and trim off the excess card. Then stick the fabric down again. If the card protrudes above the edges of the box, the lid will not close properly.

**10**

When all the sides are glued into place, allow them to dry. Then repeat the process for the box lid.

# Marketing your work

*H*ow you decide to market your work will depend on whether you approach it simply as a hobby and only plan to sell a little to cover the cost of replacing materials, or whether you intend to try and earn a living from it. The latter will not happen overnight, and to be even fairly successful, you will be faced with quite a large initial outlay of money to purchase your equipment and wooden blanks with no immediate prospect of a return. If you are a practised woodworker yourself or have a friend who is one, it may be possible to reduce these costs quite substantially.

Fortunately, pyrography does not require a large workshop nor expensive equipment. A table in a corner of a spare room with a good light source and access to an electrical socket is all the space you will need to produce your wares. Storing the wooden blanks and finished work may present you with more of a problem, particularly if you are pyrographing larger items, such as cupboard door panels. As wood is a natural material, it is affected by changes in the atmosphere in which it is stored, sometimes expanding, shrinking or warping. You must try to store the blanks in even temperature conditions, and not too dry an atmosphere. Flat items should be stored flat to avoid them warping.

While you are building up stock and getting established, you can, of course, continue with your normal job. In fact, pyrography is an ideal craft to practise in the evenings and at weekends. A word of warning! Most craftspeople who try to make a full-time living out of it do not make a fortune. Most of them earn just enough to allow them to enjoy the life-style of their choice, rather than work in a nine-till-five job. Do not make any significant changes to your economic situation unless you have done your market research well, sorted out your sale outlets and have a nest-egg to tide you over while you get established.

Selecting the range of items that you are to offer for sale is crucial, and you should undertake market research wherever you can before you make this decision. The wider the range you stock, the more expensive it becomes to keep blanks for them all. It may be better to specialize in just one area initially, for instance clocks and barometers, or small items of giftware. You can always increase the range once you are established. Visit craft fairs, and talk to other pyrographers. Look at their work, and assess its style and quality. Is it selling? If not, ask yourself, why? It could be overpriced in terms of its quality of workmanship, or it could be unappealing in its design. It may just be that the work itself is badly presented. Ask yourself, could I do better? Is your style different? Are your designs attractive? Once you have the answers, then decide what you are going to produce and how you can do it to the best effect.

## Production methods and efficiency

Obviously, you will not be able to mass-produce items, but there are ways in which you can streamline your working methods, thus allowing you more actual creative time with the pyrograph and so increasing your output. Here are some suggestions for helping you to work efficiently:

- Work on the same kind of blanks at any one time, i.e. spoons, napkin rings, etc.
- Prepare them all first.

- Trace the chosen design onto all of them at the same time.
- Pyrograph them all.
- Finish them all.
- Price them all, and pack them all.

This kind of approach involves concentrating at any one time on one process which is applied to all the same items. It does save time. If you also keep to a few standard designs that sell well, you will get much quicker at producing them. This all helps to increase output. Be methodical and organized by having everything you need to use close at hand. Assemble all the tools and materials you need to complete a process before you begin. In this way you will avoid having to interrupt your work to search for something you have forgotten.

# What to sell

The range of stock that you have for sale will change as you become better known and as you realize which of your items are more successful than others. Ideas will suggest themselves as you meet members of the public who may ask you if you make a particular item. Be careful here. Do not try to stock everything you are asked for. It may not sell well! Your bestsellers will be the mainstay of your sales and will allow you to develop more specialist and expensive items that will show off your skills to the best effect. It never ceases to amaze me how the appeal of items can vary so much from sale to sale. At some venues all the small, cheaper items will sell well. At others the larger, more expensive ones will be snapped up. The skill is always to have a stock of your bestsellers and a range of other items varying in price and showing off your skills with the art of pyrography. Remember that unsold stock is dead money. You must market items which have a rapid turnover.

# Where to sell
## Craft fairs

This is the most obvious venue that springs immediately to mind. They are held everywhere and vary considerably in the price you pay for a space,

the quality of the crafts on sale, the reputation of the organizer and the prestige of the venue. Sometimes you may earn as much from a local craft fair held in a village hall as you do at an event for which you have paid out £60 or £70 for a space and where you have sold comparatively little. It is not uncommon at larger events for craftspeople – having paid a large amount for the stall rent, spent money on travel and subsistence as well as paying for the cost of the goods for sale – to go home at the end of the day without having taken enough even to cover the stall rent. Attendance at craft fairs can be affected by the time of year in which they are held. The period leading up to Christmas – October through to the early weeks of December – is usually very lucrative. However, this is only the case if your goods are of good quality, attractively presented and priced and have sales appeal!

When selecting a craft fair, check with the organizers if there will be any other pyrographers exhibiting, and, if so, what kind of items do they sell. This will help you to avoid offering the same items for sale. Some organizers limit exhibitors to one, or at the most two, of the same craft at any one event. Also try to check if it is a genuine craft fair and not one where bought-in goods are generally for sale. This kind of fair has done much in recent years to give genuine crafts a poor reputation.

## Shops and galleries

When I first started doing pyrography in the early 1980s, I concentrated on spoons and selected designs that would be well-known in their respective localities, such as Ashness Bridge in the Lake District, The Parsonage at Howarth and other famous tourist attractions in the UK. I would take them with me when we went out for the day and I would call in at any likely looking craft or souvenir shop and show them the appropriate items. The name of the place was inscribed down the handle of the spoon. These were well-received and I used to leave them on a sale-or-return basis. The shop would ring me with further orders. It worked reasonably well. Most shops or galleries prepared to take your work on this basis will deduct a commission. Expect a sum in the region of 10 to 30 per cent to be charged and allow for this in your pricing. The advantage for the shop is that it does not have to pay out money for stock. The advantage for you is that you do not have to pay for display space or shop rental or rates. Specialist art and craft galleries may be interested in your more expensive, artistic and skilful pieces.

## Building societies and banks

With a little courage, you can approach your local bank or building society, with a view to putting a display of your work in their window. Remember to include information about yourself and your work in the display and mark the prices clearly. The bank usually arranges a suitable way for items from the window to be sold for you and pays you the balance. When I used to do this, banks did not usually deduct a percentage, but this may not be the case now. This kind of venue raises your profile locally. If you can persuade your local newspaper to take a photograph of the display and write an article about it, then it is all to your benefit.

## Tourist offices and libraries

Such places nearly always have an exhibition rota and you can apply for a space on it. My very first exhibition of pyrography took place in my local library in Longridge, Lancashire. As an avid reader, I knew the librarians very well and asked them about the possibility of exhibiting there. I was given a period of two weeks for my display and exhibition panels and cases were provided by the library. I set it up during opening hours, and the rest was left to them. The library sold the work, took the money and passed on any queries and extra orders to me. The takings were paid directly to the local council and, after their percentage was deducted, I duly received the balance. I found these occasions very successful, not only in terms of sales, but also in follow-up commissions.

## Speakers' circuits

This is another useful outlet through which your work can be sold. Other than your stock, the only expense you have is the time you spend at each speaking engagement. Travel expenses and a speaker's fee are usually paid to you. I used to give talks and demonstrations to Townswomen's Guilds, Women's Institutes, Young Farmers Clubs, National Farmers Associations, Ladies sections of the Masons and Rotary Clubs, and many more. It was a good way of becoming 'known' and provided an opportunity to sell my products. I once received a telephone call asking if a group could come and see my work. When I enquired further, I found out that it was a mystery bus tour of ladies! They had heard about me from the speaker's circuit and assumed that I had a workshop they could visit. They did come, but to the local hostelry, where we combined a meal with a talk and a demonstration!

## Artists in residence

In some parts of the country the local council appoints 'artists in residence' to their local history museums. Other organizations will also give space to local artists and craftspeople, especially groups that are concerned with the preservation of old historic houses. They tend to open such houses on a regular basis, offering a wide-ranging programme of art, music and craft events. Usually you are engaged for a week at this kind of venue. Artists in residence employed by the local council enjoy a much longer tenure. In general I have found these events financially sound, involving the minimum of expense for travel and subsistence. Again it helps to raise your profile in the area, and all the cost of advertising is borne by the organizers.

# Presentation

Without good presentation, your work will not sell, regardless of how good its quality is. You have to attract people to look, and then to buy. Here are some tips on how to display your products to the best effect.

## Tables

Some craft organizers provide at least one table in the cost of the space rent. You can usually rent another table for a small extra cost. If you have to provide your own, wallpaper pasting tables make good display units. They are light, cheap, fold up easily and are simple to carry. Two of them should provide enough display area for the average space you will occupy. If you are also planning to demonstrate, a small folding picnic table is ideal for this purpose and it means that you don't have to give up valuable display space.

## Drapes

The surface of the table will need to be covered to give your display a nice uniform appearance. If most of the work is light in tone, then choose a medium-to-dark background colour to show it off to its best advantage. Bed sheets are ideal for this purpose. They are cheap, light and easy to keep clean and pressed, especially if you buy easy-care ones! When you cover the stall, make sure that you also cover the front of it right down to the floor. As well as looking smart, it hides all your spare stock, bags, flask, sandwich box, etc.

## Lighting

Most craft-fair organizers will provide you with an electrical socket, although some will make a small extra charge for this. When you buy lighting, you need to consider how heavy it is, and what floor space it will occupy. I find the clip-on spotlights that are pivoted on a flexible arm the most useful and adaptable. They can be attached anywhere you have a convenient space in your display and angled where you want to focus the light. The cost of lights can vary considerably, but you should be able to find something to suit your pocket. Remember to take a couple of spare bulbs with you.

## Screens

Purpose-built screens can cost a lot of money. These are usually made of aluminium to save weight and are covered with various kinds of fabrics. Just as good, and costing a fraction of the price, is a home-made one, which you can make to fit your table layout. Remember when you measure the space for the screen that you must leave room in front of it so that you can stand and talk to your customers. Some of your items will need to be hung for display so your screen could be made from pinboard with a wooden frame around it. If you hinge it, you can stand it along one side of your area, then bend it at right angles and extend it along the back of the stall. G-clamps will hold it firmly in place. Finish off the screen with sealer or paint it with a colour that tones in with your drapes.

## Labelling

Price labels need to be easily seen. Most potential customers do not like to have to pick up goods and turn them over to find out how much they cost. They prefer not to ask either, in case they appear too eager to buy or become the target of pressure selling! You can use removable adhesive labels or small tie-on price tags if your items are suitable. Other useful labels to consider are ones that briefly describe the item or the technique you have used. If your handwriting is not good, then type the information and stick the caption on a folded piece of card so that it will stand up on your display table.

As a point of interest for your customers, an A4 card explaining a little about the history and the craft of pyrography could be displayed as well. It is also a good idea to leave out a few business cards printed with your name, address and phone number. People will often pick these up and contact you later.

## Other useful information

**Blocks** of any kind are very good for raising up items that you may want to highlight. These can be made of wood and covered with fabric to match your display and situated on top of your drape. I often use bricks, two or more as needed. Over these I place a piece of chipboard shelving which is obtainable from any local DIY store. This arrangement goes underneath the drape. You can probably think of other low-cost ways to enhance the presentation of work.

**Bags** Try to purchase decent paper bags. They look so much better than supermarket cast-offs! Remember the items you are selling have taken a lot of your time to produce and deserve to be put in a decent wrapper when they are sold. Presentation and a professional image is important.

**Cash box** Get a lockable one in which to keep your takings. You may also find a round-the-waist zip-bag a good place to keep your change in – far easier to get at quickly than the box. Notes and cheques can be kept in the box. It's a good idea to keep some spare labels in there too.

**Pricing** You need to stock a range of goods which fall into three main price categories. Firstly, some which sell for between £1 to £5 – cheap but attractive. People do not seem to mind spending a pound or two as an impulse buy, but they think seriously about amounts over that. The next price range runs from £5 to £15 – items in which you invested a little more time, effort and material costs. The third range of prices covers anything over £15. These will include your larger items and those which have taken a long time to complete, and for which the raw materials have been expensive. Remember most people visiting craft fairs will be quite happy to part with a few pounds but only serious buyers are going to purchase items for £20 or £30 or more. When pricing goods you need to take into account the cost of the raw materials, your time taken to complete it, wear and tear on your equipment, and overheads, such as the cost of electricity, advertising costs, stall rents, travel costs, wastage, and – last but not least – your profit margin!

**Advertising** This can be very expensive. Earlier in this chapter I suggested other ways to advertise yourself. These will take time to produce results, but they are cheap and effective. If you choose to advertise through a professional agency, then give careful consideration to your target market and the best way to reach it. If you do not give this very careful thought, the exercise can turn into an expensive failure.

**Mail order** Some of your smaller items, such as decorative or commemorative spoons, may be suitable for selling through mail order. Special spoons marking weddings, anniversaries and births, which you can trim and personalize with a suitable message as shown in Project 1, are quite easy to make, pack and send through the post. A small advertisement in British magazines such as *The Dalesman*, *Country Living* or similar publications may be worth considering. Remember to include the cost of the decoration (flowers and ribbon) and post and packaging costs in your final price.

**Special commissions** From time to time, you may well be asked to undertake a special commission. As these are one-offs, you must charge a realistic price for them. You will have to spend extra time working out the design idea and costing the raw materials. As the item is an original, you should charge more for this than you would for your standard repeat designs. It may be easier to tell a prospective customer for an original that you will work out an estimate of the price and let them know in writing as soon as you can. This allows you to work out all the costs, and give everything careful thought before you commit yourself to a price. You should also establish a realistic timescale for completion of the commission.

Above all, presentation is about looking professional. Arrive at your venue early and take your time to set out your display. Make sure the drapes are clean and pressed, your work beautifully finished and labelled. Present yourself well too, and be prepared to talk to your customers about the work, even if it does not result in an immediate sale. They may come back after looking around the rest of the stalls or they may get in touch at a later date. At all times be courteous and pleasant to the customer, however difficult this may be on occasions. Remember you need them all!

There is a market out there somewhere for you. Enjoy finding it and I wish you every success.

# THE DESIGNS

## SPOONS

# Christening plate

# WEDDING PLATE

# VICTORIAN-STYLE BOX USING SHALLOW RELIEF

# BOX
# USING SCROLLING TECHNIQUE

# JEWELLERY BOX
# USING SHALLOW RELIEF WITH COLOUR

# CLOCK WITH HERBS

# CLOCK WITH SEASIDE SCENE

# HARVEST MOUSE WITH POPPIES

# KITTEN'S HEAD

# WREN ON CONVOLVULUS

# TAWNY OWL

# A GALLERY
# OF PYROGRAPHY

Free-standing clock
(MDF with sycamore
veneer) with simple rose
design by student

Box (sycamore veneer)
with simple Celtic design
and central flower motif by
Norma Gregory

Beechwood turned bowl
with honeysuckle design by
Norma Gregory

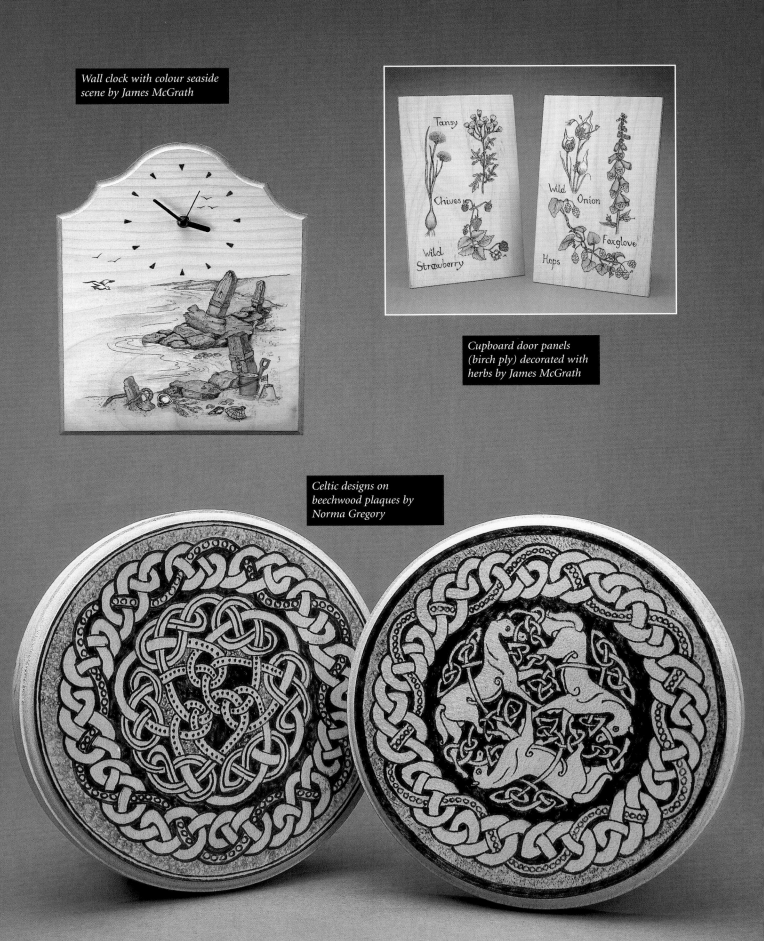

*Wall clock with colour seaside scene by James McGrath*

*Cupboard door panels (birch ply) decorated with herbs by James McGrath*

*Celtic designs on beechwood plaques by Norma Gregory*

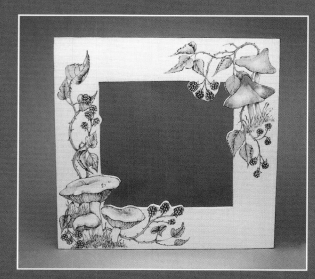

*Fungi study mirror frame
by Norma Gregory*

*Decorative colour plaque
by Norma Gregory*

*Serviette rings showing
shallow relief, line and
wash techniques by
Norma Gregory*

*Wall clock with seaside scene by Norma Gregory*

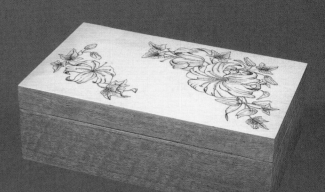

*Box decorated with lilies (sycamore veneer top with contrasting veneer sides) by Winston Graham*

*Rolling pin, board (beechwood) and spoon (hornbeam) by Norma Gregory*

*Free-standing clock (sycamore veneer) with decorative border design adapted to go round the clock face by James McGrath*

*Beechwood platter with Canada geese by Norma Gregory after C. Tunnicliffe*

*Commemorative wedding plate by Norma Gregory*

ALISON DARVILL PETER GREGORY JULY 10th 1999.

*Decorated clogs using shallow relief technique and colour by Norma Gregory*

*Framed seashore scene by Norma Gregory*

*Beechwood lined box with daisy motif by Norma Gregory*

*Coffee table designed by Adrian Admanson and made by the inmates of the Craft and Design Workshop at HMP Littlehey. Designs depicting the 'Life of Arthur' were drawn and pyrographed by Roy Hamilton. Photographed by Paul Leavan*

*Maple and mahogany veneered chess board. Sycamore veneered panels pyrographed with scenes from the Arthurian legend*

*Two of the eight sycamore veneered panels around the sides of the table. Each panel tells the story of Arthur from his birth to his death*

*Pedastal and top. The chess pieces are stored in compartments inside the table*

# ABOUT THE AUTHOR

Norma trained to be a teacher and worked initially in comprehensive schools, before moving into adult education. In time, she became Director of Adult and Community Education. In 1992, she took early retirement and resumed her artistic pursuits after a 30-year gap.

Norma became a pyrographer in 1980. She sold her work at craft shows and ran a personalized spoon mail-order service. Over the years she has given demonstrations and lessons to all kinds of groups, including women's groups, scout troops and young farmers.

Norma was recently made an associate of the British Watercolour Society and held a very successful exhibition. She has recently written and introduced the Open College Network Unit Level 1 in Pyrography. She works part of the week in an HM Prison, where she teaches a variety of design and artistic skills, including pyrography. Norma also runs an art workshop in her village in East Anglia and every year she runs weekend courses on how to paint flowers at adult residential colleges.

# BIBLIOGRAPHY

Gregory, Norma, *Pyrography Designs*,
    GMC Publications, 1999

Marks, Montague, *The Home Arts Self Teacher*,
    (c. Arthur Pearson Ltd, currently out of print)

Poole, Stephen, *The Complete Pyrography*,
    GMC Publications, 1995

Bain, George, *Celtic Art*,
    Constable, 1951

*The Arts of Woodcarving and Pyrography*,
    Butterick Publishing Company, 1893
    (collector's item, out of print)

# INDEX

# WOODWORKING

# UPHOLSTERY

| | |
|---|---|
| The Upholsterer's Pocket Reference Book | *David James* |
| Upholstery: A Complete Course (Revised Edition) | *David James* |
| Upholstery Restoration | *David James* |
| Upholstery Techniques & Projects | *David James* |
| Upholstery Tips and Hints | *David James* |

# TOYMAKING

| | |
|---|---|
| Designing & Making Wooden Toys | *Terry Kelly* |
| Fun to Make Wooden Toys & Games | *Jeff & Jennie Loader* |
| Restoring Rocking Horses | *Clive Green & Anthony Dew* |
| Scrollsaw Toy Projects | *Ivor Carlyle* |
| Scrollsaw Toys for All Ages | *Ivor Carlyle* |
| Wooden Toy Projects | *GMC Publications* |

# DOLLS' HOUSES AND MINIATURES

| | |
|---|---|
| Architecture for Dolls' Houses | *Joyce Percival* |
| A Beginners' Guide to the Dolls' House Hobby | *Jean Nisbett* |
| The Complete Dolls' House Book | *Jean Nisbett* |
| The Dolls' House 1/24 Scale: A Complete Introduction | *Jean Nisbett* |
| Dolls' House Accessories, Fixtures and Fittings | *Andrea Barham* |
| Dolls' House Bathrooms: Lots of Little Loos | *Patricia King* |
| Dolls' House Fireplaces and Stoves | *Patricia King* |
| Easy to Make Dolls' House Accessories | *Andrea Barham* |
| Heraldic Miniature Knights | *Peter Greenhill* |
| Make Your Own Dolls' House Furniture | *Maurice Harper* |
| Making Dolls' House Furniture | *Patricia King* |
| Making Georgian Dolls' Houses | *Derek Rowbottom* |
| Making Miniature Gardens | *Freida Gray* |
| Making Miniature Oriental Rugs & Carpets | *Meik & Ian McNaughton* |
| Making Period Dolls' House Accessories | *Andrea Barham* |
| Making 1/12 Scale Character Figures | *James Carrington* |
| Making Tudor Dolls' Houses | *Derek Rowbottom* |
| Making Victorian Dolls' House Furniture | *Patricia King* |
| Miniature Bobbin Lace | *Roz Snowden* |
| Miniature Embroidery for the Georgian Dolls' House | *Pamela Warner* |
| Miniature Embroidery for the Victorian Dolls' House | *Pamela Warner* |
| Miniature Needlepoint Carpets | *Janet Granger* |
| More Miniature Oriental Rugs & Carpets | *Meik & Ian McNaughton* |
| Needlepoint 1/12 Scale: Design Collections for the Dolls' House | *Felicity Price* |
| The Secrets of the Dolls' House Makers | *Jean Nisbett* |

# CRAFTS

| | |
|---|---|
| American Patchwork Designs in Needlepoint | *Melanie Tacon* |
| A Beginners' Guide to Rubber Stamping | *Brenda Hunt* |
| Blackwork: A New Approach | *Brenda Day* |
| Celtic Cross Stitch Designs | *Carol Phillipson* |
| Celtic Knotwork Designs | *Sheila Sturrock* |
| Celtic Knotwork Handbook | *Sheila Sturrock* |
| Celtic Spirals and Other Designs | *Sheila Sturrock* |

# GARDENING

# VIDEOS

| | |
|---|---|
| Drop-in and Pinstuffed Seats | *David James* |
| Stuffover Upholstery | *David James* |
| Elliptical Turning | *David Springett* |
| Woodturning Wizardry | *David Springett* |
| Turning Between Centres: The Basics | *Dennis White* |
| Turning Bowls | *Dennis White* |
| Boxes, Goblets and Screw Threads | *Dennis White* |
| Novelties and Projects | *Dennis White* |
| Classic Profiles | *Dennis White* |
| Twists and Advanced Turning | *Dennis White* |
| Sharpening the Professional Way | *Jim Kingshott* |
| Sharpening Turning & Carving Tools | *Jim Kingshott* |
| Bowl Turning | *John Jordan* |
| Hollow Turning | *John Jordan* |
| Woodturning: A Foundation Course | *Keith Rowley* |
| Carving a Figure: The Female Form | *Ray Gonzalez* |
| The Router: A Beginner's Guide | *Alan Goodsell* |
| The Scroll Saw: A Beginner's Guide | *John Burke* |

# MAGAZINES

WOODTURNING ◆ WOODCARVING
FURNITURE & CABINETMAKING
THE ROUTER ◆ WOODWORKING
THE DOLLS' HOUSE MAGAZINE
WATER GARDENING
EXOTIC GARDENING
GARDEN CALENDAR
OUTDOOR PHOTOGRAPHY
BUSINESSMATTERS

The above represents a full list of all titles currently published
or scheduled to be published.
All are available direct from the Publishers or through bookshops,
newsagents and specialist retailers.
To place an order, or to obtain a complete catalogue, contact:

**GMC Publications,
Castle Place, 166 High Street, Lewes,
East Sussex BN7 1XU, United Kingdom
Tel: 01273 488005  Fax: 01273 478606
E-mail: pubs@thegmcgroup.com**

Orders by credit card are accepted